Free Diving

FREE DIVING

A GUIDE TO UNDERWATER ADVENTURE ON THE CALIFORNIA COAST

BY JACQUES DELACROIX & ERIC MULTHAUP

CHRONICLE BOOKS

About the Authors

Jacques Delacroix is a native of France. He has dived in the English Channel, the Atlantic Ocean, the Mediterranean, the Carribean and in Hawaii. His favorite waters, however, are those of the California coast. Jacques, who is single, is a graduate of Stanford and is presently a professor of sociology at Indiana University.

Eric Multhaup, born and raised in the environs of New York City, came west to seek his fortune and settled in Northern California. Educated at Harvard, Stanford, and Boalt Hall Law School, Eric is now practicing law with Beilock, Sax and Wilson in Oakland and Martinez.

PHOTO CREDITS

Front Cover: Don Wobber, Hillsborough

L. Tan Chang, Oakland: pages 26, 34, 37, 39, 40.

William M. Goodman, Berkeley: pages 28, 54, 83, 84 (top), 90 (top), 91 (top), 93 (top), 96.

Cecil Kennedy: pages 86, 87.

Eric Multhaup: pages 27, 49, 59, 61, 63, 65, 67, 69, 74.

C. Preston Shackelford, Napa: 93 (bottom)

Don Wobber: pages 9, 22, 25, 77, 79, 81, 84 (bottom), 90 (bottom), 91 (bottom). 95.

Printed in the United States of America.
Library of Congress Catalog Card Number: 75-9294
ISBN 0-87701-062-5

Contents

INTRODUCTION

This book is about diving — about *free* diving. We wrote it because no one else had done so, despite the obvious fact that many more people are interested in diving than have been able to pursue their interest. In California alone, hundreds of thousands have been captivated by the Jacques Cousteau specials on TV. But only very few of these people have made any effort to take themselves into the spellbinding world underwater, and even fewer have kept at it long enough to learn to enjoy that world. We think this is an unfortunate waste, and we will try to explain why diving remains an esoteric activity in a state devoted to the outdoors and graced by several hundred miles of magnificent coastline.

In the following pages we will talk about diving in general; the different kinds of diving; diving equipment; places to dive; and how to dive safely and fruitfully. We will tell you what we have been telling our friends who over the years have shown an interest. When you put down this book, you should have a realistic idea of what free diving is about. And you should have been freed of certain common misconceptions about diving. Our qualifications for this task are simple. One of us has been diving for 15 years in waters all over the world, including the coast of Brittany, the Mediterranean, North Africa, the Caribbean, both Mexican coasts, Hawaii and the most favored of all these places, California, from Mendocino to San Diego. The other has restricted himself to Pacific coast diving with no regrets. We usually dive together, and we have come to a shared understanding of California

free diving through careful, systematic discussion of our respective observations. We are both amateur divers: One of us earns his living in the academic world and the other in the law. We both feel that time devoted to our vocations is stolen from the rightful pursuit of diving.

Why is diving, as we said, an esoteric sport in a state like California? We have concluded that, for most people who would like to dive but haven't, three widespread myths about diving have turned them off.

You can see for yourself how these myths take hold if you go to a popular diving spot on any sunny weekend. You can see a hundred or so divers around the beach or in the water. Eighty or more will be wearing or carrying more than $500 worth of scuba equipment. Half of these will be sporting at least $1000 worth. People who see this display of hardware might easily fall for the myth that diving requires elaborate and expensive equipment. We call myth number one "equipment fetishism." But diving need not be an expensive activity. Each of us has been free diving for the last three years with gear that we bought for far less than $100. If we include maintenance and replacement of lost items, the necessary outlay may *approach* $100, spread over three or four years, or $25 to $33 per year per person. Anything a diver spends over that sum is not necessarily useful, and usually merely complicates the diver's life (more and more expensive objects to keep track of). We'll talk more on this in the chapter on "Equipment."

If you stay and watch the divers on the beach, most of them will remind you of soldiers: their humorless, technical-looking checking of equipment, and their strut when they enter the water, will suggest Green Berets departing for a mission behind enemy lines. From their muscle-flexing and their looks of cool determination, you would think they are about to do something grimly heroic. And if you didn't know any better, you might have fallen for myth number two, "the hairy chest mystique," the notion that diving is reserved for powerfully built men and a few brave, brave women. This myth is completely unfounded in fact. True, the better shape you are in, the better you will dive and the more you will enjoy it. But anyone who can swim can do some diving. Moreover, if practiced regularly, diving will improve your physical condition. You need not be an athlete. Women do as well as men, and young children five years and over often do better than adults. As for really old divers, they never die, they just fade away very slowly. Diving demands very little brute power. And, more important, you can always limit your efforts to what you feel comfortable doing. You don't have to go in the water if it seems too rough for you. Once in, you never have to go far if you don't feel like it. We will discuss diving within limits in the chapter "Diving Safely."

If you stay on the beach long enough, you will see the warriors return, and you will see myth number three, "the empty ocean complex," illustrated. Most of the returning divers who are equipped with spearing devices, catch nets, or other devices for catching fish or other sea life will be empty-handed. If a diver does come back with fish, he will surely be surrounded by others who slyly inquire after the exact spot where the successful hunter found his prey. This "empty ocean complex," the notion that sea life is a scarcity to be caught only by the lucky few, is a major source of discouragement among beginning divers. After two or three trips during which they have seen nothing of interest, many beginners conclude that there is nothing to see and

give up. But in fact, the California coast is teeming with sea life for those who know where to look. Knowing where to look is not an instinct or a gift, but a skill that is learned. In "What to Catch and Where," we will explain how to learn it.

Interestingly, the very same people who suffer from a severe case of empty ocean complex suffer at the same time from "the sea monster syndrome" (which we will discuss in "Diving Safely"). Many people, possibly drawing from their childhood nightmares, believe that untold numbers of crawling, creeping, pouncing creatures are lurking in every recess of the underwater world, just waiting for the hapless diver to come by so they can drag him into their lairs and devour him. Naturally, if you believe that there is nothing in the sea for you to catch, and vaguely fear that something is there to catch you, you surely will not stick your nose in nooks and crannies (crevices) where sea life is to be found.

Our belief, then, is that contrary to popular wisdom, diving can be done cheaply and by ordinary people, and numbers among its rewards the opportunity of catching delicious sea food.

We would now like to speak a little about diving in general; the different kinds of diving; and *free* diving, the kind we strongly prefer.

Why Dive?

After some soul searching we arrived at a list of reasons why we love to dive: It's a fantastic thrill that's inexpensive and involves few legal risks. (You should hurry to try it, though, because it is undoubtedly psychologically addictive and will probably be banned sooner or later by federal fiat.) The form the thrill takes depends on the personality of the particular diver. For some, it is very much like a grass high — pleasant, mild, and controllable images of great variety and beauty. For others, it is very much akin to a religious experience of communing very intimately with nature. Looked at from underwater on a sunny day, the kelp limbs criss-crossing over-

Flying through the underwater sunshine is one of diving's principal delights.

head, filtering the sunrays and spreading their light to the bottom, resemble the vaults of a Gothic cathedral. For most divers, the main reward comes from moving in a three-dimensional world — flying, in other words — full of brilliant colors and fantastic shapes. In Northern California, where the underwater visibility is usually on the short side (which does not make it "bad"), you can come upon totally new scenery every few seconds. In Southern California, with clearer but less fertile waters, you can see the bottom 40 or 50 feet below and feel a sense of flying. In addition, both in the North and South, the cold water running along the diver's backbone probably causes subtle changes to muscles and nerves that contribute to the sense of thrill.

Diving is also a permanent investment in good health. Most of us know what activities are good for our bodies and systemically avoid them. On the one hand, most forms of exercise — at least, most collective (2 or more) sports — require a certain amount of organization, while on the other hand individual exercise is usually a drag. Jogging enough to make a difference, for example, requires a kind of dogged heroism. But in this age of the anti-hero most of us want to stay in good health *and* indulge ourselves. This is probably the key to success, in the long run. Diving is a great way to get into shape and stay there; you don't do it because you have to, you do it because you crave it. Possibly what diving does best for you is to shed blubber very fast, even if you don't activate yourself extravagantly in the water (and you shouldn't). Why diving has this effect has to do with the difference between the specific heat of water and that of the human body, plus some complicated physical processes we learned about in high school but cannot exactly remember. In any case, there is no way to dive in California waters without exercising most muscles quite a bit and the heart a great deal. If you smoke (as one of us does) diving will also help to clean out your lungs somewhat. We are *not* claiming that it cures or prevents lung cancer. And while you will be a significantly better diver if you *don't* smoke, if you do smoke, you need something like diving more than the next guy does. More strikingly, one of us has observed over the past 15 years (including five in the cold waters of Northern California) that diving radically cleans up the sinuses and nasal passages. In fact, we seriously wonder if steady and frequent diving is not a cure for the common cold. A diving friend who is also an eye, ear, nose, and throat doctor confirms our personal observation. One of the techniques he uses in cold-prevention research is to teach patients to sniff salt water. Diving is also a radically decisive way to terminate hangovers. Finally, it relaxes the mind and soothes the soul.

In addition to putting excitement in your life and improving your health, diving has another feature that is little appreciated. California waters are very rich in edible sealife, accessible to the moderately experienced diver. (To become "moderately experienced" may take from three dives to 20 years, depending mostly on interest and determination.) The fact is that under favorable conditions it is possible to learn how to catch abalone, the easiest of sea preys (also the most expensive to buy at the store) in two or three ocean dives.

The third great reward of diving, then, is the ability to procure absolutely fresh, high-protein food, some of which cannot be found commercially, or only at a price well above the means of your ordinary working stiff or student. And the diver who is on the hunt for abalone or other edible sea life is able to enjoy for a few fleeting moments a feeling of primitive self-sufficiency that is elating in a way difficult to describe.

With respect to diving for prey, we hasten to add that we think present California laws concerning bag limits and other restrictions are quite reasonable. An experienced diver could feed himself and a large family a very rich diet with his catch. Consequently, cheating is a grotesque, inexcusable pig-

gishness. Beyond the question of cheating there is a simple golden rule very easy to respect: Do not take more than you can use.

What dangers and hazards have we encountered in many years of free diving in California, Europe and the Caribbean? We have nothing worse to report than a few sea urchin spines in the soles and innumerable cuts and scratches on the hands. This is not to say that there are no dangers (see Safety Procedures in the Water in Diving Safely). Rather it means that, with a minimum of precautions, it is easy to avoid them completely.

Finally, the cherished common belief that California waters are dangerously polluted should be laid to rest. Except for a possible few places that may have escaped our attention, California waters are immensely cleaner than those of Europe where generations of divers have thrived and prospered since World War II without apparent ill effects. We doubt very much that any normally vaccinated individual has become sick from even prolonged contact with polluted water while diving. One reason is that because they like clear water, divers naturally prefer to dive some distance from untreated sewage outlets.

Free diving vs. Scuba diving

Diving is any activity that brings one under the water surface for any length of time. The major distinction between kinds of diving is that you can do it either with your own air or with some borrowed breathing gas brought from the surface. The first kind is called "free diving." Although there are several versions of the second kind in California it is practically synonymous with scuba (self-contained underwater breathing apparatus). Scuba divers use compressed air (not oxygen). To our way of thinking the main difference between the two is precisely that the first is *free* in more ways than one. But in this country the idea of diving has unfortunately come to imply the use of scuba (except as restricted by law, as in abalone fishing north of Yankee Point).

So strongly is diving linked with scuba that it is difficult, if not impossible, to take straight free diving lessons. This is no accident: Aside from a few YMCAs and universities, the commercial shops that sell diving equipment are responsible for the basic training of most divers. They catch the would-be diver "at birth," lead him to believe that scuba is the only way to go, and keep him tied in for life. The process is elementary: Scuba tanks require constant air refills and some repairs that are provided by the same shops. These frequent visits to the shop keep the diver informed of developments in new kinds of equipment that, for lack of a different view, he comes to regard as necessary.

More subtly, but perhaps of greater importance, the dive-shop constitutes the hub of the diver subculture, which defines what is desirable and even what is possible among divers. Here is an item of typical dive-shop wisdom: "You need scuba to catch lobster in Southern California" (false). The fact is that scuba gear is expensive to begin with ($200-$1200), and because the tanks must be refilled, each dive costs money. But, more important, because the scuba diver must visit the dive shop for each dive he is constantly prone to what we call "equipment fetishism." This vice takes three forms: buying totally unnecessary equipment; acquiring equipment that is much more expensive than necessary; and finally, replacing equipment that is still useful but no longer is in fashion or carries status. (We will examine these follies in the chapter on Equipment.) The first strike, then, against scuba diving is that it is many times more expensive than free diving.

A second very important fact should be noted: The human body was never made to breathe compressed air. Unless a series of fairly complicated precautions is taken, a scuba dive deeper than 33 feet exposes the diver to all kinds of freakish accidents. The longest dive that can be taken by a scuba diver operating at 33 feet is one hour. Past that time period or that depth, before surfacing he must go through "decompression stops" which involve sitting around in the water, doing nothing while the body readjusts. Scuba divers who operate beyond this 33-foot limit use the United States Navy Air Decompression Tables. These tables are calculated for the average Navy diver, who, it goes without saying, is a professional, and is in much better shape than even good sports divers. Even then, the Navy tables allow for a built-in 5 per cent casualty rate. So with respect to scuba, the "hairy chest mystique" has some basis in fact: Scuba diving is mildly dangerous at best, usually complicated, and often rather dangerous *and* quite complicated. What a way to relax! Needless to say, the free diver can easily reach depths of 30 to 40 feet without having to worry about these problems.

But, perhaps surprisingly, our main argument against scuba diving is neither its cost nor the danger involved, but, how it contributes to the "empty ocean complex." Using scuba is like carrying a motorcycle strapped to one's back. Out of the water it is so heavy that most scuba divers cannot visit many of the most interesting diving spots because they cannot be reached by car: Who wants to hike with a 20-pound weight belt, 15 pounds of other gear, *and* 50 pounds of tanks? Inside the water, scuba is bulky and blocks the way into every nook and cranny — where most of the action is. Finally, as we can attest after numerous hunts have been spoiled by scuba divers, the average scuba-equipped diver is as noisy as a motorcycle and warns the fish a mile away that trouble is approaching. We, too, have seen Cousteau's divers on TV doing marvels with scuba; but few of us can hope to achieve such remarkable control over our actions. In short, you will not feel like a fish in the water or be accepted as company by fish if you are blowing big bubbles of compressed air all over the place.

A question we are always asked is "How can you hold your breath underwater long enough to do anything?" The answer is perfectly obvious to us but hard to explain to anyone who has not tried diving. First, anyone can stay underwater for a least 30 seconds and easily up to a minute. All it takes is

11

practice. Second, a minute is a long time — long enough, for example, to dive into a kelp forest, drift easily over a rocky bed of brilliant underwater flora, watch the fish make polite but cautious adjustments to your presence, and closely inspect a many-rayed seastar that catches your attention. Or, there is enough time to spot a school of perch, choose one that looks particularly tasty, shoot at it, miss, shoot again, and bring the fish up. When abalone diving, if you stay in the water for two hours, you may go under 40 or 50 times, which means that you will actually spend a total of 20 to 30 minutes underwater.

For our final test of scuba diving vs. free diving, we won't try to compare the enjoyment that each kind of diving gives (although we fail to see how anybody could enjoy any recreation more than we do free diving). Rather, we simply ask who catches more of California's seafood delicacies. In all our years of diving in California we have never seen armed scuba divers return with a better catch than ours. We do not say that scuba divers never do well; we simply haven't observed any who did. There is no doubt that the Southern California spear fishermen who tackle the 600 pound black bass can only do it with scuba gear. (They also need a boat, and that's probably more important.) But a black bass is not the logical first choice of game in a diver's career.

We suspect that the habitual use of scuba hinders a diver's efforts to enjoy the underwater world, to observe sea life, and to become a good fisherman. Instead of concentrating all his senses on the underwater surroundings, the scuba diver must have his gear in mind at all times. As a result, he tends to come out empty-handed, complaining that the area has been "fished out" when in fact he has either scared the fish away, failed to see them, or simply missed them with his spear, because of the motorcycle on his back. As we said, scuba is at the root of the "empty ocean complex."

On the positive side, there is no doubt that scuba is indispensable for certain types of scientific studies, underwater still photography, and salvage work. For example, our expedition photographer, Don Wobber, has used scuba for making biological studies of sea stars, for salvaging the world's largest piece of jade from the Big Sur coast, and for photographing us. But Don uses scuba as the tools of his trade rather than as a means to relaxation and enjoyment.

It has also been argued that scuba divers are better able to catch some species like abalone — in those areas where hunting with scuba is permitted by law. True, it allows the diver to do more in a shorter period and is indeed more efficient for the capture of immobile or almost immobile game. But who cares only about efficiency? If you can get your fill of abalone or lobster in one hour of free diving, why should you want to do it in 20 minutes at a higher cost and with a greater risk to your safety?

Our choice, then, is very clear. We prefer free diving because it is much cheaper, less dangerous, and, on the whole, more effective. If you are not totally convinced by our arguments, why not try free diving (small expense) and switch to scuba whenever you grow bored with it? This has yet to happen to either of us.

1 HOW TO LEARN TO DIVE

No one can learn to dive by reading a book and going through practice motions on dry land. Some physical techniques can be learned only in the water, just as some attitudes (savvy) can be learned only through experience in the ocean. Although in the past there must have been self-taught divers (just as there are a few crazy self-taught ones these days), diving can be learned safely only from an experienced diver. There are three main sources of instruction for the would-be diver: dive shops, the YMCA, and an experienced diver-friend. Also, many colleges have diving instruction courses, but these are limited to students.

The worst source is a dive shop scuba instruction course. Such a course, consisting of 5 to 8 lessons, costs from $45 to $70 — but that's only the beginning of the expenses. And the lessons include only a minimum of free diving instruction. They also include only a minimum of scuba lessons, so *be careful* if you sign on for the whole course.* If you enroll for a scuba course, you can try to negotiate with the instructor-owner to charge a proportionate fee for only the free diving instruction. However, we have not found a dive shop that is willing to do so. If you simply sign up for the scuba course, you can complete it (shouldering the additional financial burden of $50-$60 for rental of scuba equipment for the "checkout dives") or you can drop out of the course after the free diving instruction is completed. However, the dive shop will be very reluctant to refund any of the fee. The best feature of dive shop instruction is that, possibly unlike the other two

sources of diving instruction, there are dive shops everywhere. When considering a dive shop course, be sure to call all the shops within a traveling radius you find acceptable. Get statements of costs of lessons; required rental costs, if any; whether the instruction costs will be applied to equipment purchased (your wet suit). Further, we suggest chatting with the actual instructor before signing up, to see if you feel compatible with his style of instruction and, more important, to see if you trust him. (It probably would not hurt to bring along a photocopy of the Los Angeles *Times* article mentioned and give the instructor the floor to explain why his course is not like those complained of in the article.)

The second common source of instruction is the YMCA. Because the Y and its instructors have no commercial interest in selling equipment, you are likely to get a more rigorous, less expensive course of instruction. However, like the dive shops, the YMCAs do not give any lessons in free diving alone. In the Los Angeles area, YMCAs divide their diving instruction into a scuba course and a "junior frogman" course, in which preadolescents learn to dive to the bottom of a swimming pool. If you live in the San Francisco Bay Area, you might call the YMCA's Director of Aquatics, Allen McCarthy. The aquatic programs under his direction are rigorous and thorough, and by the time you are reading this book he might have launched a course in free diving.

The third and generally the best way to learn diving is from an experienced diver of your acquaintance. Take some precautions, though: First, be

*Dive shops have earned a certain ill repute as sources of scuba instruction. See for example the front page of the Los Angeles *Times*, August 26, 1974, for an account of the shoddy standards and shady practices of many such shops, and of the real hazards of uncritically trusting oneself to such courses.

sure he is a skilled, experienced, and enthusiastic free diver. Unfortunately, while you can pretty fairly judge his enthusiasm, you can rely only on his own judgment as to his skill and knowledge. Second, friends can find the reciprocal roles of teacher and student awkward, and your friend may be unwilling to exercise the authority demanded of a teacher. He might go too easy on you, holding back on repeated, rigorous practice of the diving skills that come hard to you. Thus, you might be left half-taught, because of the friend's unwillingness to play taskmaster with sufficient determination.

Third, the friend might have little experience teaching, however fine a diver he is. Without experience in instruction, the friend could easily fail to teach basic skills that he thinks are self-evident, or that have become so second-nature by repetition in his diving that he fails to single them out for the beginner. Thus, you might receive an incomplete course.

Fourth, if the friend has less interest in teaching than you have in learning, essential corners might be cut. To minimize the likelihood of any of the problems we've listed, we have set out below a "lesson plan" for a minimum program of instruction. You should discuss this program with your teacher-friend, and make any additions that seem reasonable. But remember, everything on this program has to be learned and practiced before you can dive safely.

LESSON PLAN

The following learning program is divided into three parts. Don't think of them as "lessons": No one of them has to be mastered within a given time period. Each individual will learn these skills at his own pace, which may differ widely from one individual to the next. These differences in learning speed are due mostly to prior experience with water. They have nothing to do with bravery.

The learning steps are consecutive. It would be very foolish to attempt to move to a given step until you have those before it well under control. If you follow this advice, you will find that each part of the program is very easy and you will be amazed at your own progress. The first few steps in particular must not be skipped even if they appear a little boring. They are aimed at controlling involuntary reactions in the reassuring environment of the pool.

Lesson 1:
Learning About Essential Equipment

The most essential part of your diving equipment is your own body. It can learn to do a couple of things that you don't even suspect. Try the following experiments in the pool or any other calm, shallow, warm water.

Experiment I: Walk into shallow water and immerse your head completely. You must get your hair completely wet, even if it is going to be a mess afterwards. Blow bubbles softly and naturally. Don't hold your breath and don't exhale quickly: Remember, you have plenty of time. Then open your eyes under water. Stand up and let the water run freely across your forehead and into your eyes. Hold on to the side of the pool or any object to help you control the urge to wipe your face. This is to convince yourself that water won't make your eyeballs fall out. It doesn't even hurt; it is at worst mildly uncomfortable. Don't use your hands at all, not even to push your hair away from your face. At sea, you will need your hands for other purposes, especially if your mask gets pushed out of place. (Also, while you are doing all this, don't try to read this book. You will get it wet.)

Experiment 2: Try to sit softly at the bottom of the pool. If you don't succeed the first time and have a tendency to float upward, guess why. Obviously, you are holding vast quantities of air in your lungs. If you exhale enough, you will always go to the bottom. At the bottom of the pool, learn to lie on your back and relax; it is a tremendously unwinding experience. If you feel a little apprehensive about letting all this precious air out of your lungs, don't feel bad: You have a couple of million years of evolutionary history behind you whispering: "Don't." But remember, dolphins are not fish, either. If this thought still does not help, try the following experiment: With someone you completely trust holding your hand, exhale *all* your air (no cheating), and you will find out that you still have enough left to not breathe for 10 to 30 seconds. The paradox is apparent: The fact is that you can never voluntarily exhale *all* the air in your lungs. There is always a little left that will sustain life very well for a little while. Find out for yourself that how long you can stay underwater without breathing depends not only on how active you are while under but also on your mood. Thinking serene thoughts should easily double your staying time.

Since holding your breath comes naturally once you know everything else, this experiment is designed to help you discover something else instead: that your body is your best adjustable density flotation device. By adjusting the volume of air in your lungs you can use less effort (and therefore also less air) to go down. Practice this until you are just about able to control your buoyancy enough to stay at a chosen depth between the bottom of the pool and the surface with hardly any body movement. This step should be fun and it will tremendously improve how fast you learn how to really dive. Many divers can't stay under long enough to do any good, not because they are too slight or unathletic but because instead of dropping down exactly as fish do, they *fight* their way down.

Experiment 3:Standing or sitting in shallow water, put on your flippers. They must not make your feet ache at all at the beginning; if they do, either they are too small (if they are slip-on flippers) or the strap is maladjusted. (You don't want to hurt at all — skin diving is very sensuous.) Now place one arm alongside your body and extend the other forward, fingers loosely stretched. The extended arm is to ward off obstacles which you can't see when you are facing down, thinking of technicolor fishes. Lie down, start kicking from the hip, knees slightly bent, ankles loose, striving to keep the whole fin underwater. Practice doing this for a long time, until you are either tired or bored, whichever comes first. Don't be discouraged if your legs get tired quickly: This motion involves little-used muscles that will become stronger (as well as more shapely). Just take it easy, move slowly.

You should soon be able to swim for 20 minutes without resting. This does not mean swimming hard — a quarter mile or 30 laps is a reasonable distance — but it means acquiring water endurance. This exercise is quite different from brushing up your championship high school free style stroke. If the uninterrupted swimming time suggested above isn't coming too quickly to you don't let it hold you up. Move on to the next steps but be sure to keep practicing your fin swimming as you are learning the rest of the skills.

Experiment 4:Still in shallow water, flippers off, wait till the lifeguard isn't looking in your direction; then spit abundantly into your mask and rub it all over the internal surface of the glass plate. Rinse and repeat. Wash the outside of the plate with regular water. The spitting and rinsing is to prevent the inside of the plate from fogging up.*

Put the mask on, and put the snorkel in your mouth, with the tube tucked under the mask strap. Then submerge your head face downward, so that you are looking underwater, but with the back of your head and the open end of the snorkel above water. Breathe through the snorkel. Breathe easily.

Next, squat down so that all of your head is underwater. You will hear air bubbles as the snorkel tube fills with water. Raise yourself slowly to the surface so that the back of your head and the snorkel end emerge. Now, blow your air out through the snorkel. The water inside will be ejected like a whale's spouting. Then continue breathing through the snorkel. Repeat this step until you can clear the snorkel with one sharp exhalation on surfacing, and then resume breathing comfortably through the snorkel.

*If you are using a new mask and this routine does not help, probably the manufacturer has coated the glass with silicone. Just rub it off thoroughly with a metal soap pad.

Now put your flippers back on. Stand in shallow water with face submerged, breathing through the snorkel. Start swimming along the surface, taking easy breaths through the snorkel. Take a breath, hold it, and dive a couple feet under water, come up, blow, and swim along. Dive shallow again. This is called "porpoising." Repeat until you can make the transition from underwater to surface easily.

Go to deeper water, 8 to 10 feet in depth. Watch your instructor do a "surface dive." A surface dive is the technique for heading underwater starting from a position of floating or treading water. Try such a dive yourself. Descend until you either reach bottom, you feel like you're out of air, or your ears hurt, whichever comes first, Ascend and blow your snorkel.

If your ears hurt, try the different techniques for "clearing them," or equalizing the pressure of the water and the pressure in your inner ear and sinus cavities. First, swallow hard (with your mouth completely closed, of course) both above water and also as you dive below. If this doesn't work, pinch your nostrils shut with your fingers in the mask indentations and *gently* blow through your nose. Once the eustachian tube is cleared for air passage, the pain from differential pressures disappears. Keep trying these pressure equalization techniques. It's a knack that comes with practice. Everyone has trouble at first.

Dive in the pool's deepest area, perhaps for a penny or other object you drop to the bottom, until your ears don't hurt and you feel comfortable descending, ascending, and clearing your snorkel.

Lesson II: Diving with Full Cold Water Equipment

Rent a wet suit, hood, weight belt, and (optional) boots from a dive shop. Rates vary substantially so call around first and find the lowest rental rates.

Go to the pool with your instructor and put on your wet suit. You will feel constricted, as if you were wearing long underwear two sizes too small.

Don't worry. Just repeat experiments 1 through 4, above, with all your equipment on.

You will find that being on dry land dressed out in wet suit, weight belt, fins, and so forth will make maneuvering very awkward. So it's important to learn to move in and out of a safe pool easily and competently before you approach the ocean. Getting into the ocean often entails some tricky footwork — clambering over slippery rocks, forging through on-shore surf, and wading through kelp. On land or in shallow water, a diver in a wet suit has the agility of a beached porpoise. If you try an ocean dive while feeling constrained and awkward in your equipment, the chances of some small obstacle frightening you are seriously increased.

One suggestion for saving money: If you rent the equipment for your practice dive on a Friday, you can practice Friday or Saturday and make the first ocean dive on Sunday for the single rental fee. Rental rates are usually the same for one day or for one weekend.

Lesson III: Your First Ocean Dive

In Northern California, the best place to take your first ocean dives is Monterey Bay. Two traditional baptismal beaches are next to the Outrigger Restaurant, in Monterey, and the Cannery Row breakwater. Both places are flat, safe, teeming with divers, yet full of underwater scenery and fish.

In Southern California nothing beats the La Jolla Cove. (See the chapter discussing "Where to Dive" in detail.)

On your first dive, you should be scrupulous in practicing the techniques, customs, and habits we discuss in "Diving Safely," even though Monterey Bay is invariably safe and often looks like a bathtub. Get accustomed to the ritual of watching the ocean for a good while, making salty comments about the wave action and currents, and plan your dive according to the placement of rocks, kelp, and waves.

If your instructor friend is to teach you properly, the first dive should be a total bore for him. He should show you by example the aspects of Pacific Ocean diving that cannot be learned in a swimming pool. (That week of snorkeling you might have done in the Caribbean doesn't count, either.) Here is a checklist:

- Getting into the water over a rocky beach and through surf on the shore
- Swimming out to deep water over rocks and kelp
- Diving in kelp and surfacing in a kelp bed
- Diving to the bottom, holding onto kelp as an anchor and really looking at things
- Keeping aware of how far from shore you are, where you are drifting, how tired you are, etc.

For this lesson, you *must* make an agreement with your friend that you can ask any question during the session and that he will answer to your satisfaction. Nothing that makes you the slightest bit nervous in the water can be left unexplained, because a lurking worry creates its own danger.

After you practice simply diving in salt water and surfacing, with the friend watching very closely, relax and enjoy the colors and the feeling of flying. If it's a sunny day, you turn onto your back underwater and watch the sunbeams spread among the kelp. A touch of paradise.

Lesson IV: Setting out on your own

Lesson IV is the same as lesson III, except that you act like this is a normal nonlearner's dive. While your friend should spend 90 percent of his energy keeping track of you, he shouldn't hover. This is the last practice dive, so ask any questions, admit any fears, and mention any reservations you have. After this, you might be diving for abalone in rougher waters, with less visibility, and in rockier areas. If you don't feel comfortable during the final check-out dive, you will be in serious danger of becoming frightened and panicky when you dive in open water. So, remember that Monterey and La Jolla are beautiful, safe places to learn, and you should instill in yourself safe techniques, attitudes, and habits.

After these four lessons, you are a minimally competent diver. If you don't *feel* competent, restrict your diving to Monterey or La Jolla until you do.

2 DIVING SAFELY

It is difficult to write about the hazards and risks involved in diving. Most diving experts are self-styled (as are we), and each of us is bound to have his own ideas about the potential dangers in diving. No doubt the assessment of each diver is also colored by the enthusiasm he feels for diving: The greater his delight, the less he is likely to yield to fear. Therefore, as divers trying to introduce you to a sport we feel passionate about, the best we can hope to do is to give you our own, honest reckoning of the dangers, as we see them, and of the ways of avoiding or preventing them.

One pitfall we hope to avoid in our account is the "hairy chest" mystique — the suggestion made by many that they are heroes for ever venturing into the treacherous, monster-infested waters of the Pacific Ocean. Granted, sharks live in the ocean, and granted, a diver may sometimes see sharks, it is tempting to overemphasize such a danger just to appear a teeny bit brave. (It beats bragging about the last time he got seasick because of the previous night's drinking bout.) You will see that the most serious dangers that divers face are their own errors of judgment and carelessness.

First, keep in mind that as long as you are *free* diving, you are breathing natural stuff — your own air. This in itself frees you from 90 per cent of the perils popularly associated with diving. Free diving does not expose you to the "squeeze," the "bends," nitrogen narcosis, or any of the more exotic ailments associated with the breathing of compressed gases.

The dangers of free diving should never be confused with those associated with scuba diving. (as you can see from the statistics at the end of this chapter). On the one hand, free diving is more dangerous than ordinary ocean swimming *only* in that it may take you into waters where you would not ordinarily choose to swim. But on the other hand, you are much better equipped than the regular swimmer to foil whatever tricks the ocean might have up its sleeve. Your wetsuit is at once a very effective flotation device and very good protection against scrapes and bruises. The flippers help carry you far with a minimum of fatigue. The hood shields your head from cold water and the mask protects your face.

It can never be repeated enough: There is no such thing as water "karma" or simple luck. Being safe is all a matter of learning, and anyone can learn if he allows himself to. The dangers of diving, in our view, fall into two categories. Both categories are real, but the first is overemphasized by its appeal to vivid imaginations, and the second is too often overlooked because it may seem tedious and technical. Sea monsters and exotic creatures seem far more dramatic fare than do precautions to be taken to protect us from ourselves and from weather conditions.

SEA MONSTERS AND OTHER FISH STORIES

The ocean has inspired many myths and stories about terrifying dangers for people who place themselves on, in, or near the water. For the free diver, most of these notions are without foundation. There is no need to worry about man-eating sea monsters, spiny corals with lethal stings, or overpowering riptides and undertows. We will discuss several of the sea-monster legends simply to dispel them for what they are, and to give a few safeguards against the small kernels of true danger at the core of each fairy tale.

Octopus and Squid

Probably the most fear-inspiring underwater animal is the octopus, with its comrade-in-terror, the giant squid. In California, octopuses are shy, retiring creatures. They might leave their place of seclusion under a rock to investigate a diver, but never to attack him. Further, California octopuses are much smaller than the giants of Puget Sound. We have never seen an octopus in California waters while diving, and, while searching for ling cod, cabezon or abalone, we have looked in exactly the places where octopuses would be likely to live. We have stumbled across them partially exposed during very low tides. To get one out from under its rock takes tremendous efforts. If you grab an octopus, it will most likely grab back, and a tug-of-war ensues. The octopus can really hang on. Therefore, our advice to the free diver is: In the extremely unlikely circumstance that you see an octopus underwater, don't grab it. If this rule is followed, there is no possibility of danger.

Small squid can be seen in Southern California, swimming freely near the surface. These present no danger. Large squid very seldom and only accidentally inhabit waters that the free diver is likely to use.

The Dread Shark

Next to the legendary giant octopus, the most feared sea creature is probably the shark, the subject of abundant folklore and recently some scientific literature. The shark's somewhat ugly features might contribute partly to its bad reputation. On the other hand, there is no doubt that sharks present *some* danger to divers, although not much more than to ordinary swimmers. Sharks do occasionally attack and kill people. Shark attacks have been filmed and photographed; and human remains have been found in the stomachs of captured sharks. A very small number of extremely gory shark stories have been engraved in the collective memory of Californians, and while they should be taken seriously, they should not keep you out of the water.

We must give this subject more attention than we think it deserves because every spring the media can be counted on to spread pointedly alarmist horror stories about sharks. For example, the June '74 issue of *Esquire* had a spectacular piece about sharks. After surveying the numerous modern ways of being "done in," it concludes that sharks are the only "true horror" left. One could argue that it is all very much a matter of personal taste.

Since we cannot, as few can, claim to be very experienced with sharks, we did some research on this delicate topic. However, since rigorous scientific shark studies are very recent, everything said about sharks must be taken as tentative. This is what Jacques Cousteau had to say about sharks in 1950: "The better acquainted we become with sharks, the less we know them, and one can never tell what a shark is going to do.*

By way of comparison, this is what Lineweaver and Backus state in their excellent Natural History of Sharks.**

In *Chesapeake Science* in March 1967, Schultz analyzed 1,406 attacks dating from the middle of the last century to the present. He found that sharks attacked on sunny days, on stormy days, in clear water, in murky water, in daylight, in darkness, in estuaries, in bays, in rivers, in lakes with an outlet to the sea, in the sea itself and at all times of year; that sharks attacked at water temperature as low as

*Jacques Cousteau, with Frederic Dumas, *The Silent World,* revised edition. New York: Ballantine Books, 1973.
**Lineweaver & Backus, *Natural History of Sharks.* New York: Anchor Books, Natural History Ed., 1969, p. 70.

53° F, but that the great majority attacked at water temperatures above 68% F; that 50.1% of unprovoked attacks occurred within 200 feet of shore and some within five feet; that 69.8% of those people attacked without provocation were killed.

The lesson is a plain and simple one. Attack can occur almost anytime and anywhere. But it occurs most often, as one would expect, when and where the most sharks and the most people occur. That means in the summer season in temperate regions and all year around in tropical ones. Most attacks in United States waters occur in Florida but there have been incidents all along the coast, from Swampscott, Massachusetts, to Trinidad Bay in Northern California.

The same authors cite *thirty-two* reported unprovoked shark attacks on swimmers, divers, waders, surfers, and waterskiers over a period of four years (from 1962 to 1966) and for the whole United States. That's an average of eight per year for the whole country. Putting together the two statements, we find that the great majority occurs *elsewhere* than in our Golden State where the water temperature is apparently too low. This leaves us with an absolute maximum of three unprovoked shark attacks per year, on all kinds of people who spend time in the water — skin divers and everyone else. In fact, an estimate of one or two per year is probably closer to the truth and still somewhat high.

Contrast this figure with the statistical danger of just staying home. Say you live in Los Angeles: Just staying put will increase your chance of becoming the victim of one of the 600,000 to 700,000 crimes committed there annually. If you don't like staying home, you might want to go for a nice, quiet weekend drive. There are no sharks on the road — but of course there is always the chance that you will join the thick ranks of the 50,000 odd people injured or killed in weekend automobile accidents each year.

In point of fact, for males between the ages of 15 and 34, motor vehicle accidents and homicide together account for nearly half the deaths. If you happen to belong to that group, almost anything you can do that keeps you away from internal combustion engines and your fellow human beings is sure to prolong your life. (If you are a female in that age bracket you are in slightly less danger.) We could go on forever citing statistics, but the thing to remember is that real risks ought to be treated as real, — no more, no less. We *do not* recommend seeking sharks out, pulling their tails, and making obscene gestures at them.

Once you have reduced the dangers presented by sharks to their true proportions, there are a few things you must learn. In Northern California, the few shark attacks in recent years have happened at Point Reyes, Tomales Bay, and San Francisco Bay, all places accursed with waters that are exceptionally murky because they are close to the outlets of large rivers. In Southern California, where sharks are either more visible, more plentiful, or both, the La Jolla coast has a bad reputation, probably mostly undeserved. The closeness of La Jolla to the edge of a very deep marine canyon may favor the presence of large sharks that would not otherwise be found there. Data for the area between Santa Barbara and San Diego are hard to come by, which is probably a good sign that nothing bad has happened there.

Most diving manuals are directed to scuba divers, and routinely offer advice that is of little use to the free diver — don't blow too many bubbles; don't thrash about in the water; and if you see a shark, don't turn your back on it. For the free diver it is more useful to remember to surrender what ever catch you have to the shark's benefit and then swim slowly to shore. In general, you should attach your catch to a fairly long line dragging behind you. Don't carry *any* fish on you if you suspect you might be in a shark area. Since we tend to believe that the probability that a creature will attack another creature underwater has a lot to do with their respective size, we add to this list: Stick with your buddies. It will make you all look bigger and more impressive.

Cousteau believes that sharks are dangerous but rather cautious about what they eat. His crews rely for their protection on the shark billy, merely a broomstick with a few nails at the end, sharp points facing outwards. The shark billy is not used to hurt the animal — a nearly impossible feat — but merely to convince it that the diver is poor fare and to keep it at a proper distance from the diver.

We have never had any real problems with sharks for two principal reasons: First, we dive mostly in rough waters which they don't seem to like; Second, we dive mostly in Northern California where we would not see them if they were around. One of us has never seen a shark in the water. The other has had fewer than fifteen glimpses, including extensive diving in tropical waters. On his first sighting, off the coast of the Yucatan Peninsula, in Mexico, he just slavishly followed some of Cousteau's early advice and put to flight two man-size sharks by shouting at them. On another occasion, in the same region, a 10-foot blue shark rushed by him without so much as wasting a glance. The only time an encounter with a shark felt like a close call (though it probably was not) was off La Jolla one day during a very hot summer. Having swum alone (always a mistake) to the kelp beds about half a mile from the beach, the imprudent young man shot a large perch with a big (five foot) air gun. A four-foot shark immediately dashed out from nowhere, seized perch and shaft, jerked the whole set loose from the gun by breaking the line and made off for the depths from whence it came. Reasoning correctly that if one shark showed up within seconds of the shooting of game, there must be many sharks around, including large ones, the discomfited diver swam back to shore sadly holding onto an empty gun. It should be noted that this incident happened in very calm waters on a very hot day, during a summer in which sharks were particularly numerous in Southern California. (Small sand sharks were literally moving about between the legs of bathers standing in shallow water.)

Our own steps for minimizing the dangers of sharks are as follows (these are *our* steps, not the *only* ones):

- We are always on the lookout for potential dangers
- We plan reasonably well in advance what we would do depending mostly on its size, if we encountered a shark
- We will sacrifice our catch to any potentially dangerous shark *without any hesitation.*
- We believe that if the miniscule risk of meeting with a hostile shark kept us from diving, our overall fate would be worse — we would be more overweight, weaker-hearted, and more cholesterol-clogged than we are now.

But this has to be a personal descision.

Barracuda

Another large predatory fish, the barracuda, is sometimes (wrongly) charged with the nasty work done by sharks. We are convinced with Cousteau that "barracudas are no danger to divers."* Their impressive beauty, their tenaciousness, their intelligence, and their furtiveness have given barracudas a somewhat devilish reputation among experienced spear fishermen. The beginner may confuse the veteran's respect with fear.

For a diver, the barracuda is just about the most desirable game fish because while it is fairly easy to find (and to attract), it is extremely difficult to catch, and it is fit for a king's table. In areas where spear fishermen and barracuda have operated alongside each other for a while, the barracuda have undoubtedly learned to recognize the fishermen and to use them. Though they are rarely seen in Southern California, in warmer waters barracuda will follow spear fishermen at proper distance (out of gun range) and swiftly seize any improperly speared fish. A fisherman's first experience of being shadowed by a pack of 15 or 20 sharp-toothed four footers** would make him understandably nervous.

*Cousteau, p. 181.
*The Pacific barracuda almost never exceeds this length, with a weight of 10 to 12 lbs.

Spider crabs (above), jellyfish, and sea urchins afford no danger to the diver who knows how to touch them.

After a short while, the diver realizes that the fish have no hostile intentions toward him and he will either ignore them or become obsessed with bagging one.

Eels, Jelly Fish, and Others

About moray eels, most lobster catchers have frightful stories to tell — most of them hard to believe. Most people find morays, with their vicious snub faces, remarkably ugly and repulsive. They live in holes (often shared with lobsters) from which they seldom emerge except at nightfall. While they do have very sharp teeth and tend not to back off if provoked, they do not attack divers or anything very large. The rule is: If you don't mess with them, they won't mess with you. We know of no moray eels north of Santa Barbara.

Jelly fish of several species abound all along the California Coast during the summer months. While some species inflict painful stings if handled, divers are adequately protected from contact by their wetsuits. Also, because jelly fish are highly visible in the water and, needless to say, do not lunge, they are easy to avoid. Jelly fish are also very beautiful creatures, and close observation of their translucent and colorful bells will show you another of nature's miracles in the raw.

California sea urchins have spines no sharper than the teeth of a comb; they contain no poison or toxin, and needless to say, they can't shoot their spines. On the other hand, female sea urchins contain a delicious batch of eggs, rivaling caviar in delicacy of taste. California sea urchins can be easily and safely handled with bare hands.

One other animal is bound to cause alarm on first sight. This is any member of the seal family, which includes sea lions, sea otters, and sea elephants. These are intelligent, curious, and playful animals, which often seek out the diver for inspection and

22

apparently for amusement. While some seals are quite large, and present an imposing sight when cruising on the surface or underneath, there are no verified incidents of any harm wrought by a seal on a person. On the contrary, these creatures are playful and amusing.

Of all the animals to be found in the ocean, the most dangerous to the diver might very well be his fellow man. The first danger posed by man should be obvious. Nevertheless, every year there are a few accidents involving divers and spears. This is totally unnecessary. Just strictly observe three rules:

- In waters where you cannot see as far as your weapon will reach, never fire a spear gun if you don't know where your diving companions are. They might be behind the fish you are aiming at. This sounds absurd, but we know of one case, in the crystal clear waters of Yucatan, where two divers, aiming at the same barracuda, shot each other simultaneously. Think of the embarrassment of having to explain such episodes to your friends.

- Never point a shooting device at anyone or in anyone's general direction, whether you believe it is loaded or not. This elementary rule applies even more strictly in the water, where visibility is often poor and fingers are sometimes numb.

- Finally — and it is surprising to see how many experienced divers ignore this rule — never, never enter or leave the water with a loaded or cocked gun. The reason behind this rule should be apparent: Entering or leaving always involves moments of imbalance which are a perfect occasion for inadvertently spearing yourself or a buddy. For the same reason, never lean on any spearing device while putting on or removing fins.

Fellow humans constitute an additional hazard to the diver when they are motorized. There is nothing more terrifying when you are underwater than the buzz of a fast-approaching speedboat. Fortunately, this never happens in abalone diving since abalone are almost always found in tumultuous, rock-spiked waters shunned by speedboat hotrodders. In the calm waters within or near the mouth of a harbor, the speed of boats is normally strictly regulated, giving you plenty of time to get out of the way. If you are diving in calm open waters in a frequented area such as most of Monterey Bay and much of the La Jolla coastline, you can still help yourself: Attach a red and white diver's flag to your float. Hope that it will prevent the hotdog with the twin Merc 80s from buzzing through your vicinity. Pray.

Kelp

One form of marine life generates more anxiety among beginning divers than any other: kelp. It is difficult to say whether this anxiety is realistic or not, and we will discuss the problems of kelp below. One thing is certain: While the chance of encountering a dangerous shark or moray or giant squid is exceedingly remote, the probability of having to deal with kelp is about 100 per cent. This is because kelp is the most reliable, most visible sign of a good diving spot. Fish congregate in its upper and middle reaches. Its presence indicates a rocky bottom providing homes for abalone and bottom-dwelling species of rock fish.

The California kelp is nothing but a kind of seaweed, but a seaweed of such unlikely size as to be a major component of the diver's environment. A kelp bed is typically composed of any number of lithe "trunks" rooted into a rocky bottom, or sometimes anchored on loose rocks at the bottom. Each trunk spreads out into ribbonlike branches at or near the surface. It is common for the branches of one strand of kelp to mix with the branches of another, forming a floating mat of varying thickness. The lower reaches of each trunk either are completely free of lateral growths or bear very short, thin minor limbs which do not mix with those of adjacent trunks. Each trunk may easily be thirty or more feet long (or tall).

Beginners are often frightened of somehow becoming tangled in the kelp. Are the grounds for this fear real or imagined? Is it yet another instance of sea monster phobia, in which the kelp will perversely reach out and *grab* the hapless diver? Or is this fear a healthy assessment of a real potential danger? Possibly most divers' fears of kelp combine healthy caution with morbid imagination. We used to believe that kelp presented no danger whatsoever to the cool diver. We used to believe that all of the very few accidents occurring in kelp could be traced to the victim's own destructive, panicky actions. Then we changed our minds, each of us separately but almost simultaneously, in the course of an unusually hot, sunny summer in Northern California. The heat and light had caused floating mats of tangled kelp beds to grow much thicker than usual. Each of us came up from the bottom and could not break through the matted surface. This happened only once to each of us in many years of diving, but once is enough — and maybe one time too many if you're not prepared for the problem. We were forced to take the unpleasant step of diving back down and searching out an open spot while feeling very short of air.

As is nearly always true of any source of danger in the ocean, the problem of giant kelp can easily be solved with appropriate techniques. The technique used depends largely on where the diver is in relation to the kelp bed; swimming deep underwater through kelp is different from swimming near the surface. Swimming underwater among trunks of kelp involves no difficulty since there is little or no lateral growth below the surface to slow progress — it is rather like walking through a pine forest, dodging trees.

There are two ways to cross a kelp bed: the first involves treading and crawling; the second involves "porpoising." The least tiring way is also the most difficult to master, though anyone can learn to do it, little by little. You push the kelp ribbons away from yourself where the mat is thin and crawl over it where it is thick. The main unpleasantness of this way is the risk of losing one's weight belt. (On the other hand, crawling on the surface of water and kelp involves a special thrill because it is an entirely new locomotive experience.) The other way to cross a kelp bed is "porpoising." You repeatedly dive to the level that is free of branches, swim as far as possible underwater, and surface for air. It gets to be rapidly tiring. It also involves the rare but real danger mentioned — the danger that the surface kelp mat is too thick to breach. Whether you are porpoising across a kelp bed or whether you are actually hunting fish or gathering abalone inside a kelp grove, you will have to break through that surface canopy. Rarely is the surface matting too thick to be broken through or even to break with one's hand, providing one precaution is taken. The precaution is simply that before coming up for air, you aim for an area of the canopy through which the surface of the water itself is visible. This may sound obvious and self-evident , but both of us had grown so confident that kelp could always be broken through that we had fallen into the habit of coming up anywhere at all. Usually, the edges of a kelp bed have the thinnest mat; these are good places to begin getting used to choosing one's breakthrough spots and practicing actual breakthroughs. Swim up with your free hand extended upward and spread the kelp with it before your head reaches the surface. Usually, you can descend through kelp by a normal surface dive, one hand holding the buckle of your weight belt to prevent loss.

Don't be afraid of kelp; learn to use it.

In sum, the danger presented by sea creatures is minimal, far smaller than the danger of driving between home and beach. We feel certain that of all the divers who are injured in diving-related activities, nine-tenths are hurt in auto accidents en route. The irrational fear of underwater predators is extravagant compared to the actual danger involved. If people inflated the actual dangers of driving cars as much as they do the actual dangers of octopus, sharks, and the like, our highways would soon be used only for roller-skating.

Kelp groves look like underwater jungles to the new diver; gradually they become more like a magic forest.

Safe Diving Plans:
The Ocean, the Weather, and You

Now that you no longer consider the ocean filled with sea monsters of all varieties, we turn to the only two significant sources of trouble, the condition of the ocean surface, and the diver's own physical condition. The most important part of safe diving takes place out of the water, when making the decisions first whether to dive and then where to dive.

The decision-making process begins at home, a few days before you plan to go. You gather information about weather and ocean conditions. For example, if you live in Northern California, you pick up the *San Francisco Chronicle* first thing in the morning, take the second section, and without even glancing at Herb Caen, you open to the weather section. Read the paragraph titled "Pt. Arena to Pt. Conception." Suppose it says something like:

Winds mostly northwesterly 5 to 15 knots. Seas 2 to 4 feet with northwest swells 2 to 4 feet. Mostly fair with late night and early morning patchy fog.

Then you are in business for diving anywhere, so long as these conditions hold. However, if the report tosses around such phrases as "small craft advisory" or "seas 8 to 12 feet," you should restrict your diving plans to Monterey Bay.

In Southern California, check the Los Angeles *Times* Marine Forecast for "Point Conception to the Mexican Border." Suppose it says:

Light variable winds night and morning, becoming westerly 10 to 15 knots with two to four foot wind waves this afternoon. One to two foot southwesterly swells through tonight. Mostly fair with night and morning low clouds.

Conditions are right. If the wind is higher or the ocean is rougher, better stick to either protected

A typical predive conference, with Eric pointing out where the big ones live and Jacques listening dubiously.

places or indoor sports. It doesn't hurt to call a dive shop just before you plan to go diving and ask if any divers have given them reports about visibility and roughness. Such late reports are useful because it is very difficult to predict the condition of the ocean from even the most complete weather forecasts. You must be prepared to adjust your diving plans when you arrive at the ocean, and even have other plans in mind if conditions turn out to be unsuitable for diving at all.

We have established a ritual that helps us to make this crucial decision when we arrive at the beach. Our group gathers and faces the ocean, and salty comments are exchanged about getting back to the sea, feeling the maritime air in our citified lungs, and so on. Then someone begins talking about wind direction and velocity. Everybody should say something on the subject, not necessarily profound, but simply to be sure that each person is aware of the dimension of the wind factor.

Then someone notices the size of the swells and the surf. Swells are the steady rollings of the ocean; surf is the very end of the swells as they break near the beach. It is possible to have big swells but small surf, and vice versa. Further, the size and pattern of both should be watched for several minutes, because waves generally follow cycles that include both large ones and small ones. At the calm point in the cycle, you can glance at any apparently flat ocean and overlook the dangerously rough action a few minutes later at the opposite point in the cycle. When you have observed a full cycle, then reflect on the observations you have made. As a rule, swells pose no problem to the diver (except for inducing seasickness in some); he simply bobs up and down like a cork. On the other hand surf poses the biggest danger to divers. Large waves crashing on a rocky beach are very difficult to negotiate, whether entering or leaving the water. Thus, heavy surf pounding on a rocky beach is a sufficient reason not to dive.

White water breaking in the open ocean away from the beach indicates real turbulence and requires caution.

Now, most diving spots have some surf right on the beach. The difficulty is deciding what surf is manageable and what surf is dangerous. Experience is the only help when close decisions are involved. For beginners, we offer the following rule of thumb: If the surf begins breaking (that is, you can see white foam as the wave finishes its roll and crashes over) more than 20 feet from the water's edge, it is too rough to dive. When the swells are so powerful that they break such a distance from the end of their roll, they are too powerful to permit inexperienced divers to enter or leave the water easily and safely.

If you have noted the size and location of swells and surf and have found them tolerable, then plan your dive: you choose a place to enter the water and a likely-looking place to dive (kelp beds are the best indication of good diving); you watch the direction of any current or wind; and you choose an alternative place to land in case it is difficult to return to your entrance point.

Currents describe only the surface motion of the ocean; they do not include undertows, riptides, or any other bugaboos. The only time a current can "sweep away" a diver is if he is in a channel during a change from high tide to low tide. The open ocean might have cross-current, which are only swells coming from different directions because of a change in the wind direction. Cross-currents make the ocean choppy — that is, give the diver more bobs to the minute while he is on the surface. Also, the wind and current can cause you to drift, but this is nothing like the popular notion of being carried out to sea. You compensated for drift by checking landmarks every few minutes or so, and either swimming back to your chosen diving spot or planning to land at your alternative beach down current. We suspect that very few divers are carried out to sea by overpowering waves or currents. Unfortunate incidents occur not because of powerful tides or currents, but because divers get into water that is

27

Crawl all the way out of the water.

clearly too rough for them, frighten and exhaust themselves, and then are carried out by small currents or tides. You are most likely to exhaust yourself during an attempt to get out of the water onto a rocky beach with large surf breaking over you. You get knocked around, can't hold onto anything, and get scared and tired. Watch out for big surf breaking over rocks. In addition, when trying to get out through surf, never stand up, even in shallow water, because your feet will get tangled up and a wave may knock you down. Rather, swim and then crawl all the way out.

When you and your friends have observed the ocean and wind conditions and have found them hospitable, and a good plan has been made that each member of the group feels comfortable with, your safety in the water is virtually assured. Of the few diving accidents that happen, most of them are caused by mistakes made on dry land. In acceptably calm water with careful people, diving is very safe indeed.

But one further decision must be made: Are *you* fit to dive safely? Each diver faces possible trouble spots that can make him dangerous to himself and his diving companions. Late nights and carousing before the dive leave you weak, easily tired, and prone to seasickness. A flu or other germ which produces the same symptoms of tiredness and nausea should keep you out of the water.

Even if you feel physically normal when you arrive at the beach, take the following precautions. If you tend toward carsickness or airsickness, you probably also tend toward seasickness. Take dramamine or its equivalent a half hour before diving, and in the hour before diving, eat little.*Burping and barfing are really unpleasant in the water, and you often sip in salt water. Plus, a nauseous diver is virtually helpless to swim back to shore, navigate through waves, or do anything other than want to perish on the spot.

So, the group must first decide whether ocean conditions permit diving, then each diver must de-

*If you feel you need some food for energy, try Fig Newtons, honey, or other light quick-energy foods.

cide whether his physical condition permits diving. Remember that even if you don't feel like diving when you arrive, you might feel more like it later. At least you won't feel worse because of a bad experience in the water* These two decisions, made on dry land, are the keys to a safe dive.

SAFETY PROCEDURES IN THE WATER

Diving is intrinsically more dangerous than most other types of entertainment in the following sense. A person drinking beer and watching television risks nothing worse than a headache; a tennis player risks nothing more than a fall on the courts or aching muscles from overexercise. But a diver can drown — and some do each year. However, the risk of drowning can be reduced to almost zero. Diving is thoroughly safe if, first, each diver scrupulously follows safety procedures and, second, each group of divers consciously and cooperatively does the same. Moreover, as a free diver you are safer than the scuba diver, since you have no mechanical equipment to fail you underwater.

Your diving instructor will explain the usual safety precautions. But in addition you can both be and feel safe and comfortable by making some extra efforts. In the buddy system of diving, each diver has a partner with whom he remains in close contact underwater and for whom he shares responsibility. This system works only if each person in the diving group, shares an equal commitment to safety. It takes only one clown in a group of divers to disrupt a dive by ignoring the agreed-upon safety procedures. Suppose the hot dog in the crowd swims off on his own to explore an eye-catching coral formation without telling his budding. The buddy notices he is alone and feels both unprotected himself and worried about his missing buddy. He stops his fishing or browsing and starts a fast search of the area, because if someone is in trouble, you have to act fast. It is unnerving to conduct an underwater search in an atmosphere of worry and fear for a buddy. The searcher may take risks to search as far and as fast as possible. If others in the group are called in to aid the search, their diving is also interrupted and the spirit of the day is lost.

If the errant diver returns, exclaiming "Oh wow, you should have seen this far-out stuff I just saw," wait until everyone is safely back on shore to forcefully explain the trouble he caused by his breach of safety. If the trouble-maker is not thoroughly penitent, or if he makes an excuse or attempts to minimize the trouble he caused, there is only one remedy: Never dive with him again. For each diver in a group to be safe, every diver must be equally committed to practicing safety.

Since collective agreement among divers in a group is essential, we have developed some worthwhile conventions. First, it is difficult to communicate in the ocean, especially in the murky waters of Northern California. Often you can't see your friends underwater more than 10 feet away, and in surface swells you can't see them above the water since everyone is bobbing up and down on different cycles. So divers must stay close enough to see each other. If you are right next to someone, you remove your snorkel and talk to him. But if you are five or more feet apart, you need signals. Since there is no universally accepted set of hand signals used by divers, each group has to agree on its own particular code. Most hand signals can just be common sense gestures, but you should be careful that each is different enough to be distinguished underwater, and often under adverse conditions; for example, "waving" can have several meanings ranging from "Hey, here I am and doing fine," to "Come here, I want to show you something interesting," or "I'm in distress, come here at once."

For the crucial signal, "Help," the water safety committee of the International Skindivers' Association has proposed the following rule for international acceptance: No diver shall raise both arms above the head unless he requires immediate assistance. This applies to communication among div-

---

*Needless to say, indulging in a couple of beers or a joint before you go in, for whatever purported reason, is very, very dumb.

29

ers, as well as from diver to shore, or diver to passing boat. It would be comforting if all divers acknowledged this "two arms up" emergency rule.

One final safety point: Any diver *must* have the right to get out of the water at *any time*, without pressure to stay in longer than desired. Trouble starts when a diver starts feeling a little tired, or a little seasick, but decides to brazen it out for fear of cutting short the group dive or acting like a poor sport. Since a tired or seasick diver is a risk, the rule must be absolute: Anyone can return to shore any time, with a cheerful escort if that seems appropriate (and it usually is if there is surf breaking on rocks at the shoreline, or if the departing person shows any signs of uneasiness).

An account of the only time a member of our group got "in trouble" will show both the cumulative violations of the safety consciousness which led to the trouble and how easily it could have been avoided. On a cold, nasty 16th of March, three of us set out on the ritual "opening of abalone season" dive. After hiking over a cold, wet path, we found a very rough sea, with four or five-foot waves breaking regularly in shallow water. Our first mistake: we decided as a group to dive, in spite of unfavorable conditions, because it was the first day of abalone season. Our second mistake: The least experienced diver decided to include himself in the group, although he had never dived in such rough water. We suited up, and the relatively inexperienced diver was lent a safety flotation vest, which he had never used before. Our third mistake: This piece of equipment was improperly put on and wasn't checked by the more experienced divers.

We swam out into the surf, which is ordinarily no problem because you can easily dive under each breaking wave and come up in the ensuing calm. But so tightly had the flotation vest been tied that the diver couldn't take in a full breath of air. He was forced to continually dive underwater to escape the breakers without having enough air in his lungs — a very unpleasant situation.

The diver asked his buddy to try to loosen the vest, but this could not be done in the surf. The fourth mistake: The uncomfortable diver failed to call it quits immediately, inform the others, and head for shore. Instead, he painfully waited a couple of minutes until, once the severity of his predicament was understood, everyone agreed to go in. By this time, he was feeling an acute shortness of breath and was very tired and thoroughly uncomfortable. He dropped his weight belt to provide greater buoyancy, and unhappily made the "long swim in" between the two other divers, who guided and encouraged.

Clearly, none of this should have happened. But it could have been much worse. We emphasize that taking any chance that increases the risk of drowning is inexcusably stupid. Further, being in trouble in the ocean is very frightening and can easily lead to panic.

As with everything else about diving, popular beliefs about the safety or dangers of diving are more fancy than fact. Hard facts are very difficult to come by: After serious research, we could come up with only one trustworthy report on diving safety — and it is only tangentially related to free diving. Since in a particular area there is no good way to keep tab of the number of divers — particularly free divers, who do not need to be certified — the evidence in this report can not be regarded as conclusive.

Around 1971, the Los Angeles County Underwater Safety Committee published a document covering approximately the LA Metropolitan Area coastline. The report included 63 fatal diving accidents between 1965 and 1970. In only two of these were the victims free diving. One free diving victim was 47 years old and very experienced. There were indications that he had speared a fish that was so large it was carrying off his equipment; the diver apparently had overstayed his bottom time cutting the line. The other victim was 17 years old and also said to be experienced. He had been diving continuously for four hours; just prior to his last dive, he had stated that he was tired. Both victims were alone in the water at the time of their accidents.

While the 61 scuba diving drownings don't relate directly to us, the circumstances of these drownings can be instructive. An incredibly high proportion of the victims had a known past history of cardiac or respiratory illness. Of the several divers who had been drinking, some *also had heart trouble!* A majority had failed to drop their weightbelts when they encountered difficulties. In a few cases, the flotation vest worn by the victim was thought to have been a direct or indirect cause of drowning. Believe it or not, several of the victims had entered the water with tanks and weighbelts *but no fins!*

The general impression left by this report is that almost all of these accidents could have easily been avoided. Recent evidence (see again the August 26, 1974 issue of the Los Angeles *Times*) places the chief responsibility for such mishaps on the sloppy training given in scuba instruction courses by dive shops. Simple *competence* is the single most important element of safe diving. Anyone can learn to dive safely, but it must be *learned;* there is no shortcut whatsoever.

A final word of caution: We know from experience that fairly young children (say those as young as 11 or 12) can learn to skin dive quickly and well. However, one should never forget that they have not reached their full muscular development. So, whatever their level of competence and experience, they should be taught to tailor their dives to their limits of strength and stamina. In particular, *never* compare, even implicitly, the performance of one child with another or with adult divers. Such comparison could well produce foolhardiness in a young person eager to prove himself a better diver.

3 EQUIPMENT

If you have chosen to go free diving, most of your expenses will come in one big chunk, when you buy your first set of gear. Fortunately, the pain involved can be reduced considerably if you buy rationally — if, that is, you protect yourself from the Christmas shopping effect of the diving shop, and if you know what equipment you really need, and of what quality. To help you in this task, this chapter is divided into two sections: essential equipment, and optional equipment. (The second section cannot be complete because innovations are continuously appearing on the market.) Finally we will examine *some* of the superfluous equipment found on or about the persons of California divers.

This is a good place to do justice to dive shop owners, who have been presented so far in these pages as heartless mercantilists. You will find most of them to be helpful, competent, and personable. And if you are in a place foreign to you, they are often the best or only source of information about where to dive. But you have to remember that your interest and theirs do not coincide exactly: Yours is to keep costs down; theirs is to sell you enough stuff so that they can retire early to dive off a Caribbean island. Remember also that they have much more practice at pushing their interests than you have at defending yours.

In buying your gear, two major ideas must guide your choice. First, except for your wetsuit, every piece of gear you take in the water is very likely to be lost before it is worn out. Second, every moving part is a source of potential trouble. If you would rather become a good diver than a competent water mechanic, buy simple stuff. Both ideas point toward cheap equipment. We will illustrate as we go along.

The Wetsuit

It is an inescapable fact that everywhere in California, in any season, the water is too cold to dive without a wetsuit. Even in San Diego, where the air gets very warm in the summer, any dive below 10 feet will send you back shivering to the surface. Because the wetsuit is at once your major expense and the most essential piece of equipment, it must be carefully chosen. This can be made fairly simple by grasping a few facts. A wetsuit is a one or two-piece garment made of synthetic rubber. A diver's wetsuit (not to be confused with the surfer's variety) covers the body from ankle to neck. To it is usually added a hood made of similar material unless the suit itself includes head protection. The suit restricts the entry and slows the circulation of water in direct contact with the body; this layer of water trapped inside and heated by the diver's own body protects him from heat loss. That is why it is called a "wet" suit. There are also drysuits, which prevent entry of water altogether and trap a layer of air instead. Though they tend to be even more effective than wetsuits at heat retention, they are also more expensive and are very fragile. Thus, they should be avoided by the beginner.

Clearly, the wetsuit should fit the body very snugly. In fact, out of the water, a good wetsuit should slightly impede breathing. The main problem in wetsuit shopping is to find a cut that does not form pockets in various places; it should really fit like a second skin. Slightly overweight men in particular must make sure that their suit does not form a loose pocket over the small of the back. A few quarts of cold water permanently located at the base of the spine can be very uncomfortable. Good stores will carry several brands all cut a little differently. It is mandatory to try them all before buying. Better yet — and this is what we recommend — it is worth the expense and trouble of renting several suits before buying one. There is no better way than by actual use in the water to find what fits your particular configuration. Be sure to note the measurements and type of each wetsuit you rent so that you remember which to buy when the time comes.

Women will encounter slightly more trouble in finding the right fit, whether because their anatomies vary more than men's, or because women buy too few suits to make it worth finding a few "standard" cuts to fit them, or because of institutional sexism. A woman who does not find the right suit for her in the women's section will sometimes find it advantageous to search the men's section if she is on the large side, the children's section if she is small. The latter solution also has the added attraction of being inexpensive.

When all else has failed (which is very rare) both men and women must consider the custom-made suit. Unfortunately, the true custom-made suit bought from a shop costs about twice as much as the ready-made kind. An attractive alternative is to buy by mail order. Some catalog and diving publication ads include detailed measurements to be sent to the manufacturer. Such a "quasi-custom made" mail-order wetsuit costs about the same as a ready-to-wear store-bought one. The only inconvenience is the delay involved.

The second most important consideration in buying a wetsuit is thickness. Here again the rule is simple: the thicker the better. In Northern California, ¼-inch thickness is mandatory; south of Santa Barbara, you can probably get by with 3/16-inch.

Everything else about wetsuits is a matter of taste, finances, and option comfort. Most wetsuits today include a nylon lining whch makes it easy to slip them on and off. While this is certainly a welcome amenity, we prefer using the old style ones to save money, even if we have to carry a box of talcum around for the on/off maneuvers.

Also, more and more one-piece suits have an attached hood and "farmer John" cuts that provide a double layer of rubber around the torso. Both are undoubtedly superior to the old two-piece garment for cold protection, but they are more expensive and are not absolutely necessary. However, if you are determined to splurge, the wetsuit is the best place to do it. For one thing, you are unlikely to lose it in the water.

Every wetsuit gives you two additional benefits: First, it protects you from bruises and scratches. Second, it is an excellent flotation device. With your suit on and without a weightbelt, you should be able to float on your back in the water, arms and legs up, holding your ankles with your hands, head raised. Try it sometime — it's fun.

Other Necessary Equipment

Hood The hood insulates from the cold some important organs useful for thinking; it also restricts water circulation along the spine. Get one, even if you plan to dive in Southern California. It's nice to know you have a kind of helmet on. The hood may be of thinner material than the suit.

Mask The simplest, cheapest masks are also the most trouble-free. They include a single, flat glass plate with no valve. The shop man will tell you of the advantages of the valve (blow out any water that creeps in). These advantages, real or imagined, are more than offset by the fact that a valve reduces the sturdiness of the mask. This is generally where

This is Jacques with the six essential pieces of equipment: wetsuit, weight belt, flippers, hood, mask, and snorkel.

water starts seeping in. If possible, your mask should be black; rubber articles of other colors include a colorant that makes them more brittle. The rubber should have one indentation on each side of the nose that enable the diver to pinch the nostrils shut without taking the mask off, in order to equalize pressure in the ears. For a price, corrective glasses can be fitted inside a mask. If you want this done, inquire at a shop before you buy a mask; it is well worth the expense.

Snorkel Again, the simplest are the best. A snorkel should be straight at the end opposite the mouth; the mouthpiece must feel comfortable. All fancy contraptions that include ping pong balls and other stoppers, as well as snorkels incorporated in the mask, are potentially dangerous and should be avoided. Fortunately, they are becoming rare.

Flippers About this piece of equipment, we are in complete disagreement with the general California practice. Diving schools almost unanimously rec-

ommend the "Navy" type of flipper, which is heavy and rigid and has an adjustable strap that leaves the bottom of the heel exposed. Though we doubt it, this type of flipper may have some advantages for the scuba diver. But for the free diver, they are utter nonsense. Because flippers are the first thing you will lose in the water they should be cheap ones; the Navy flipper is expensive. The Navy flipper's rigidity and weight make taking off and landing in heavy surf very hazardous to the ankles of the average diver. Its weight in your pack discourages hiking to diving spots off the beaten track. Its adjustable strap is the perfect example of the moving part that always causes trouble or breaks at the wrong time. The fact that it leaves the heel exposed forces one to use booties (see below), an added expense. Its only possible advantage is speed (and the corresponding disadvantage of fatigue), but we are convinced that there is never any reason to move fast in the water. Indeed, one of the main beauties of diving is the grace and relaxation of buoyancy, which has nothing to do with speed. For all these reasons, we recommend that you get a soft, lightweight, nonadjustable flipper that encloses the heel completely. Such a flipper is called a "slip on" or "step-in" flipper. One final note — you might want to try a "jetfin" type of flipper. While these cost more than $20 a pair, they are designed to deliver more thrust per kick. They have the adjustable strap mentioned above. We don't use "jetfins," but we freely admit that we have heard no complaints about them.

Weightbelt The human body's natural tendency is to float; so is the wetsuit's. Put the one into the other and you are an unsinkable cork, bobbing helplessly up and down on the water's surface. If you want to dive rather than fool around on the surface, you must have a weightbelt. It is a quick-release belt, for safety, on which lead weights are strung. Any quick-release belt, including a discarded automobile safety belt, will do. Weights sold commercially come in a variety of shapes and sizes. It's good to have some small ones to make minor adjustments suited to the kind and depth of diving you do. Many shops will lend or rent molds with which to make your own weights from discarded lead. Note that it is not absolutely necessary to use lead; lead is merely the most convenient of metals because it melts at a low temperature, provides much weight for little bulk, and does not rust and is therefore clean. Experiment if you wish and let us know what you find; we are eager to find a substitute for the commercial weightbelt because it is expensive and easily lost. Some Mediterranean coral divers go down holding a big ingot of pig iron in their hands. The ingot is tied to a surface float or boat by a long line. When the diver is ready to go up he just lets go of the ingot and pulls it up later from the surface. This might work for abalone diving.

How much weight you need depends on several factors including your own bodyweight, the shape and size of your wetsuit, and your own personal coefficient of floatability. Your instructor should advise you as to the proper amount. To cross check, tell the dive shop man what kind of a suit you have and ask him how much weight you will need. He will want to be on the safe side and indicate a number below the proper one. Try it, and the next time around add more according to your first experience. Chances are that you will underweight yourself consistently. For one thing, out of water it is a major exercise to carry your belt, weighing between 15 and 25 pounds. Just remember that, contrary to your secret apprehensions, coming up to the surface is not very difficult; on the other hand, you will waste a lot of your energy and air just fighting your way down if you are insufficiently weighted.

Optional Equipment

Booties A variety of ankle-high booties made of synthetic rubber or nylon can be found in dive shops. They conserve body heat and are desirable with open heel flippers. But they're just more equipment to keep track of — and to lose. Besides, they are fairly expensive.

If you have followed our advice about flippers and if you find that you get cold too fast, wear a pair of heavy woolen socks, which are much cheaper and do about as well. We prefer to wear the flipper directly on the skin.

Gloves Synthetic rubber gloves retard heat loss. They also protect from scratches. But we prefer to feel what we are doing, especially in murky waters. Diving bare-handed allows for a better grip on whatever we are holding; this is particularly important if what we are holding is a $20 to $50 gun. We always come out of the water with scratched hands (good for the "hairy chest" mystique) but have not once become infected from such scratches. If you are a little squeamish at the beginning, especially when diving for abalone which involves a lot of hand contact with rough rock, wear garden gloves. Chances are that you will lose them and never bother to replace them.

Life vest We doubt that life vests do more good than harm to *free* divers. When you think you are in trouble (which should happen rarely or never), you should drop your weight belt; your wetsuit is enough by itself to keep you comfortably afloat. But a badly rigged life vest may become entangled in your belt and prevent you from jettisoning the belt.

Abalone iron If you live in Northern California, the first game you will probably want to go for is the abalone. Though it is entirely possible to catch abalone with bare hands, it takes a little practice, and at the beginning you will need a tool to pry them off the rocks where they live. "Ab irons" sold commercially are not terribly expensive ($2.50 to $10), but are not very good either. You might just as well make your own. An abalone iron must strictly conform to the legal specifications described in the next chapter, "Free Diving and the Law." Other than that, to be effective, your iron must be very thin (1/8" to 1/4") and tapered at its working end. It must be very sturdy, as a mature, smart abalone well-ensconced in a crack can offer a lot of resistance to your detaching efforts. Finally, while it is good practice to carry your tool tied to your wrist, it is also a good idea to be able to get rid of it easily because it is entirely possible to get it stuck in a crack 20 feet below. The best solution is to drill a hole in the handle of the tool and to thread a piece of rubber or surgical tubing through it, tying the ends together to form a loop and then tying the loop to fit the wearer's wrist fairly snugly but not tight enough to cut blood circulation. If your iron gets stuck, you pull with your caught wrist, to stretch the diameter of the loop, and use your other hand to keep the loop expanded while you slip the caught hand free. Getting your iron or even your hand "trapped" by an abalone is a rather far-fetched possibility, but since we have heard stories about such things happening, we tell you what to do just in case.

Catch nets A variety of nets and bags are sold commercially. Aside from allowing you to look professional, we can't figure out what their superiority is over any old gunnysack. If you can't buy gun-

nysacks at your local coffeehouse for 25 cents apiece, ask your local grocer for a couple of the nylon net bags used to transport onions. Each one will last for about three or four dives and will be suitable for any kind of game except the largest fish. If all else fails, steal a pillow case from your grandmother (grandmothers usually hoard too much of this kind of stuff anyway). Note that you need a catch net or bag only if you go after scallops or lobster. All fish can be strung on a piece of line or wire through their gills and mouths. Likewise, nature has thoughtfully endowed abalone with small holes along one edge of their shells through which a wire coat hanger can be strung. One of us almost never carries a bag but instead strings abalones and fish alike on a coat hanger held in the left hand.

Guns and spears If you intend to go after any kind of fin fish, you will need some sort of device. This involves a relatively large expense and must be given a great deal of consideration. Unfortunately, it takes a while to try different kinds of devices on different species of fish, and it takes some time to become good enough to decide what one's needs are. So read carefully and follow our simple advice.

This first thing you must know is that the all-around, "good for everything" gun has not been invented and is unlikely ever to be. However, you can find a weapon that comes close to it for any particular marine habitat. Find out where the best local fishing is and equip yourself for that particular area.

If you live in a region of California where abalone is fairly plentiful (anywhere North of Big Sur and many places South), don't even think of buying a gun until you are good at catching abalone. This will give you time to take in the typical scenery of your area and to observe its marine animals casually. If you only have access to a less fortunate place, try to find some substitute (rock scallop, lobster, crab) that will give you an excuse to dive and do the same. We maintain that you have to have "an excuse," because we have observed that divers without one usually get cold and bored before they have had

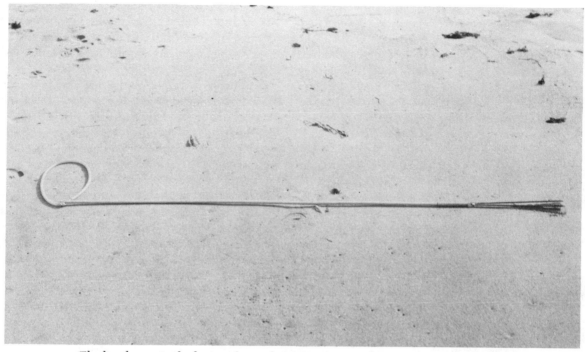

The handspear is the best, safest and cheapest weapon for spearing fair-sized fish.

time to become acquainted with their playground. In addition, until you become a little skilled in the water (see the chapter "What to Catch and Where"), searching the bottom for fish to observe is an excellent way not to see any and to catch the "empty ocean complex" prematurely.

In Northern California, visibility is on the short side even on the very best days. If any of the shy species of fish are around, you never see them and you might just as well forget about them. Thus, in this kind of marine environment, the *ability to shoot far is unimportant.*

In the southernmost part of California (San Diego and environs) the water is very often clear and shy species abound. In this kind of water it is nice (but not mandatory) to own a weapon that can truly reach out.

These considerations, as well as your budget, should dictate your choice of a spear. If you live near the Central California coast, the choice becomes more difficult. You should decide what your local conditions are most like, and choose accordingly. Remember, though, that there is no way to make a truly terrible choice: A good fisherman can catch fish with a slingshot.

If your area is one of murky water and brazen fish, you want a weapon that is cheap and easy to carry and to reload. Ease of reloading is essential because in such waters you often get several chances at the same fish, while in clearer waters a fish missed will often "hole up" for the day. Your needs will be well met by the so-called hand spear, a light fiberglass or aluminum rod with a spearhead mounted at one end and with the other end carrying a rubber-tubing loop. Your hand both aims the spear and acts as the trigger. To shoot, you simply let go of the rod while retaining a light grip on the loop. This sounds complicated but, actually, anyone can learn to do it in a few minutes. With a little practice, the whole movement takes less than a second.

Whether you decide to buy a sling or make it yourself (which is easy), choose a rod between four and five feet long, absolutely straight and smooth surfaced. The loop can be made of surgical tubing, which has a high resistance to salt water. The best all-around head is a long (5 or 6 inches) flaring trident. This trident must not be confused with the "Neptune" trident, which is flat and the prongs of which are arranged in a line, like the tines of a dining fork. We can't figure out how Neptune got to be king using such a clumsy device. The flaring trident has three prongs which originate at the same point, thus:

If, on the other hand, you have access to clear water, the diving ground for shy fish hunting, you should seriously consider buying or making a true spear gun. As usual, the main thing is to know what *not* to buy. There is plenty to tell, but we will keep it short, just remember not to consider anything that is not mentioned here until you are old and experienced. First, avoid any spear that propels shafts with a force provided by anything other than rubber; don't get a compressed air gun of any type or one using CO_2 cartridges, unless you are a gun freak who actually enjoys cleaning, greasing, caressing, and worrying about weapons. Such devices are uniformly fragile and expensive (the worst combination for a low-budget diver).

The second pitfall is the toy gun, thousands of which are sold every year. Anything under three feet in length (two and a half at the very least) is a toy that can't shoot anything. Beginners often buy them with the fallacious reasoning that they must be acceptable to learn with. The fact is that short guns are inaccurate and pack no power. It is probably better not to have a gun than to own a toy gun: If you have *no* gun, true, you don't catch anything; but if you have a toy gun, the fish laugh at you and demoralize you. So you want a gun long enough to offer accuracy and power, but not long enough to impede your movements and be clumsy to load.* Three to four feet is about the right length. Unfortunately, most inexpensive guns sold commercially have bodies made of aluminum, which tears fairly easily; steel is preferable, while fiberglass, a sturdy plastic, or wood are even better. The rubber bands that come with commercially sold guns are universally too long or too thin or both — that is, they're not powerful enough. This is no big problem, since most shops will make them to order or you can make your own at small expense with surgical tubing. Your next care is the shaft, and there you have a problem: American-made guns come equipped with steel shafts that are much too thick and heavy for speed and accuracy. Unless you shoot point blank, you can see the shaft glide gracefully toward the bottom as it moves away from you. The fish see it, too, and sail on by. One solution is to order a gun from Europe or have a friend bring you one. Although an expensive and/or complicated solution, it might be worth it in the long run, because the French, for example, converted to the so-called Tahitian arrow, and anyone who has tried it does not want to come close to the old clumsy type. The Tahitian is essentially one long, thin shaft made of a very lightweight alloy. It is simply sharpened at one end and includes a single movable barb which at rest lies completely flat against the shaft. The other extremity has a single notch on which to affix the metal part of the rubber band. This shaft flies extremely fast with improved accuracy. It also tends to bend more easily than the old type when maltreated, and even if restraightened shows a great loss of accuracy. Since the Tahitian shaft is cheaper to manufacture than the old kind, Europeans don't mind much. But the extra cost involved has to be considered by a Californian who would depend on shipments from abroad. An additional problem is that so far Tahitian arrows come only in metric sizes, which means that you are also forced to buy a European metric gun. In spite of all these complications, you should still consider this solution because Europeans — the French and Spaniards particularly — make guns that are better and less expensive than either American of Japanese products, at least in the inexpensive, beginner's range.

*You will need a long (5 or 6 feet) gun for big fish such as grouper or barracuda, but you have time to think about that.

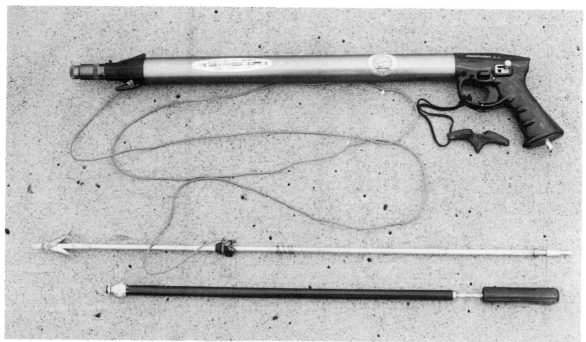

Compressed air speargun. The black device at the bottom of the picture is a pump analogous to a bicycle pump. The gun needs to be pumped only a few times per year. It includes a button to let air out, thus controlling force and velocity of shot. The small butterfly shaped object right underneath the handle is used to force the shaft into the gun barrel against the resistance of the compressed air. We do not recommend this kind of weapon or any other compressed air spear gun because they are costly, fragile and difficult to repair. For the meticulous diver only.

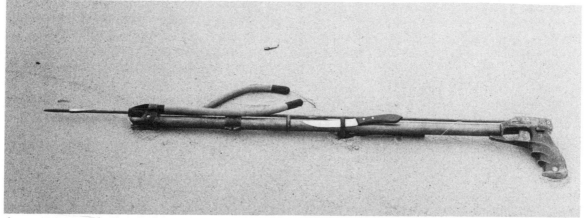

Ordinary (3 feet) rubber band arbalete in uncocked position. The lighter spot along the barrel is the blade of an ordinary steak knife strapped to it for emergencies. This is the kind of weapon we recommend. It is easy to care for and contains few moving parts. The length, strength and thickness of the rubber bands can be varied without limit to control force and velocity of the shot. The arbalete in this picture is of French manufacture. The barrel is plastic and the handle aluminum. It is equipped with a "Tahitian" shaft.

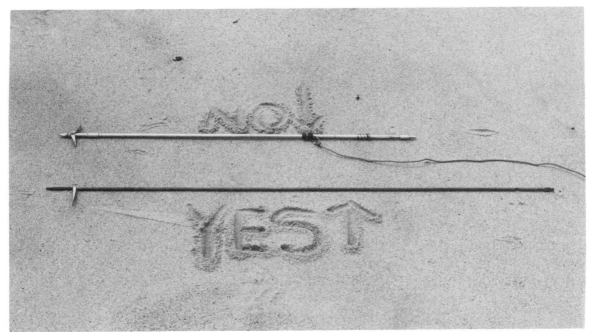

Compare the light, slim, one-piece "Tahitian" shaft with the clumsy projectile which accompanies most factory-made spear guns. The "Tahitian"shaft is a faster and more precise missile, but requires more care in retrieving speared prey because it has only one barb.

Bigger guns Large fish are not only more powerful than small ones, they also tend to be smarter and more wary. (That's how they got to be big in the first place.) Consequently, hunting big game (more than 15 pounds) almost demands a larger gun (6 feet or more) that will provide the force necessary to penetrate deep into a large fish, and the speed and accuracy for long shots. Large fish have the wisdom to stay away from anything resembling a gun and when speared they can shake themselves loose with incredible strength if not shot right in the head. Here again, the best choice is a rubber-band gun. Since there is no limit to how much you can alter the length, width, and number of the rubber bands, you can always pack enough power for any fish. A big gun should be equipped with a sturdy shaft ending in a detachable head that is made of two parts: a ring firmly screwed on the end of the shaft proper and a sharp part which slides into it and rests there. The two parts are connected by a piece of

strong plaited wire about three inches long. When a fish is speared, its first movements cause the point to slide from the ring; from that moment on, its convulsions are transmitted to the flexible wire rather than to the rigid and heavy shaft, thus avoiding the tearing of flesh that often results in a well-speared fish shaking itself free. Such a head is a little more expensive than the standard ones but it is well worth it. Nothing is more heartbreaking than seeing a carefully stalked and neatly speared thirty-pounder run away!

A last word of advice on the versatility of a large gun: While it is true that within reasonable limits, it is quite possible to spear small fish with a large gun, remember that the larger the gun the more cumbersome, the longer the reloading time. In close-range shooting, such as when hunting in holes, a large gun makes it impossible to get close enough to the holed-up prey to shoot with accuracy.

Finally, guns and spearing devices should have

40

some buoyancy. In free diving, a diver rather frequently shoots a fish when he is at the extreme limit of his bottom time. In such a case, and if the victim is small enough, it is good policy to let go of everything and to come up for air. In any area with lots of kelp or nooks and crannies or both, it often takes considerable time to retrieve even a properly speared fish. A floating gun, once let go of, will shoot straight up toward the surface, to the limit of free line, not entangled in weeds. When you come down again to get your tool and fish, it will be standing there, several feet above the bottom and well in evidence. A hand spear will tend to go right up to the surface and lose the fish. In both cases, it beats searching the matted tangle of weeds at the bottom for a tool that may have been dragged quite a way by the wounded fish. A number of firms manufacture floating guns, but any ordinary gun can easily be made floatable by tying a piece of styrofoam near the handle. For similar reasons, it is a good deal to paint your gun handle yellow or to attach a piece of bright-colored, salt-water-resistant tape to it.

Knives Divers' knives range in price from $8 to over $60. They are the joke of the century and the perfect expression of the "hairy chest" mystique. Worn strapped around the leg, they seem to suggest that sharks had better stay away if they know what's good for them. The fact is that no knife will so much as scratch sharkskin. In any case, if a shark comes close enough to be stabbed and he has evil intentions, your best recourse is to regain quickly the faith of your childhood and pray. In all seriousness, we know of only one sure use and one possible use for a knife. In spearfishing at great depth, a speared prey sometimes holes-up so tightly that it is impossible to retrieve. In that situation you may have to abandon fish, shaft, and gun to their fate — that is, unless you carry a knife that you can use to cut the line connecting shaft to gun, thereby saving the gun. The second use of a knife is hypothetical. We have not yet found a good way to pry off big scallops; it is entirely possible — but not guaranteed

— that a strong knife is the best answer. Note that neither use requires you to own a "diving knife." Buy a dozen used, stainless steel steak knives at a Salvation Army store. Keep one at the bottom of your bag if you use one. Or make a sheath out of anything and tie the sheath to your belt. Another solution is to strap it with a rubber band to the tube of your speargun. Of course, after a few dives, each knife will start rusting, even if you keep it well greased, but since the dozen will have cost you less than the cheapest, worst-quality diving knife, you are still way ahead of the game. This is especially true if you consider that the average diver loses his knife rather rapidly.

Floats A float is any floating object used to support the diver and/or his catch while in the water. Floats come in three categories: the rigged up inner tube ($3-$5), the souped up air mattress ($17-$25), and super-surfboard ($250). Besides its outrageous price, the last has the gross defect of being so heavy that it can be transported only by car. It actually looks like an extralong, thick fiberglass surfboard with neat little compartments in which the diver is supposed to place his gear. It may have some usefulness for the scuba diver who wishes to dive a couple of miles from the coast. For the free diver, such a float belongs in the realm of immobilizing, superfluous objects: Once you own such an expensive piece of equipment, you feel that you must use it, and pretty soon you find yourself limited to those spots which are accessible by car.

The second category, a short air mattress of sturdy material with a few feet of holding line attached, is OK but unnecessarily expensive. It does nothing that a small inner tube won't match. Some people like to rig up a tube with an elaborate decking of burlap and bags. We prefer to simply attach a line to ours so that it can be tied to floating kelp when not in use and so that a catch bag can be hung from it.

Note that though it offers an added security, a float is not absolutely necessary; one of us almost always uses one, the other almost never.

Backpacks and Other Carryalls Though the weightbelt is best carried around the waist and the spearing device in hand, everything else must go in a bag while on land. If possible, the bag should be large enough to carry both your equipment and your catch. Remember that five medium-size abalone are not only bulky but heavy. It is also convenient to have pockets available in which to permanently keep spare pieces of line, shaft heads, sharpening stones, rubber bands, etc. For all these reasons and because we prize our mobility, we favor the old style (Boy Scout) canvas backpack. (The new jazzy nylon ones seem too fragile to use on sharp rocks and rough terrain.) Try other solutions or adopt this one, but this is surely not your first order of priority. One of us simply carries all his equipment to and from the beach in the same gunnysack used as a catch bag while in the water.

Care of Equipment

If you are concerned to be frugal in your purchases of equipment, you probably want it to last as long as possible (that's true only if you have renounced from the beginning the satisfaction of being stylish. Fortunately, taking good care of your gear is very simple; it requires only a little routine discipline.

All of your gear has three main enemies: salt, sun, and cracks. Rinse everything thoroughly with fresh water after each dive; don't leave it in the sun; and don't fold your wetsuit. The last piece of advice, addressed to you overzealous types, is particularly important. If you fold your wetsuit, you tend to do it always along the same lines; pretty soon, nice creases will develop into unfixable cracks. The best rule is to have no rules and to just roll it as it comes or to spread it flat.

With respect to the first command, don't panic if you are without fresh water for a day or two after a dive; your gear will not break up instantly. Just do it as soon as it is convenient. Likewise, it is good policy to fix any hole or crack with neoprene cement as soon as it appears. It is easy and very effective (as good as new). It is also a good idea to wash a wetsuit by hand with a little soap once or twice a year. Given a modicum of care, your wetsuit, which is the most fragile and most expensive part of your equipment, will faithfully serve you for a long time. For three full years, one of us kept an old-style, unlined suit bought for $40. Counting a minimum of 150 dives during this period, this comes to about a quarter per dive! A hand spear demands no care other than rising its rubber loop as you would any other rubber part. It helps to lightly grease the mechanism of a spear gun once a year. Some gun handles (where the mechanism is located) can be split right in the middle by removing some screws. If you have such a gun, open it, put some machine grease inside, and use the opportunity to place a piece of styrofoam (for flotation) inside the handle. If you have a riveted gun, just stuff some grease through the shaft opening with a knife or a piece of wood. If you don't grease your gun, also rinse the handle after each use while pressing and depressing the trigger to get all the potentially corrosive salt out.

In any case, don't get infected with equipment fetishism, your gear is more likely to be sturdy than not and it is supposed to serve you, not you it!

4 FREE DIVING AND THE LAW

Divers can run afoul of the law in two typical ways, one in the water, the other on land. The first way is by violating the Fish and Game Department regulations about catching various sea animals; the second is by trespassing on private property on the way from car to beach. The first potential trouble spot can be avoided entirely by knowing and scrupulously following the Fish and Game regulations. The problem of public access to the beach, on the other hand, will be a source of conflict for many years to come. However, we will suggest below several ways of dealing with beach access for the near future.

Fish and Game Laws

First, however, the "easy" problem of the Fish and Game regulations needs a little explanation. Each year the Fish and Game Department publishes a booklet of rules that govern the "taking of any fish, mollusk, amphibian or crustacean in California waters." A violation of any of these rules is punishable by a fine of $35 to $500, or six months in jail, or both (Section 8001 of the California Fish and Game Code). This booklet can be obtained when you get your fishing license, which costs four dollars at most dive shops and sporting goods stores. The rules are written in rather complicated legal-bureaucratic jargon, and are filled with tricky double negatives, exceptions, and other irritating marks of an "official" publication. In essence, the rules state the size and number of each kind of

animal that may be taken, and how and when they may be taken. However tedious, the safe approach to these rules is to read them carefully and obey them. This is not really a great burden, as there are sound ecological reasons behind most of the rules, as well as the obvious legal-bureaucratic authority.

Since virtually all Fish and Game violations by divers are related to abalone, we will explain exactly what the abalone rules mean and how they are applied by game wardens at the beach. First, "Every person while engaged in taking [any kind of fish, including abalone] . . . shall have on his person or in his immediate possession whatever license is required for the taking of such species." Obviously, you can't take your fishing license underwater with you but it is better to take it to the beach you actually dive from than to leave it, say, in the glove compartment of your car, particularly if you hike a distance from your car to the diving spot. It would be within the discretion of the game warden to let you go to your car to get the license, but it's not worth risking $25 to count on the warden's being in a benevolent mood.

Read the rules about ocean fishing; the regulations effective through February 28, 1976, place the following conditions on abalone catching: Open season is March 16 through January 14; the possession limit is five abalone. This does not mean that you can catch five abalone on each dive, or five abalone on each day, and accumulate them. It means that you can never have more than five abalone in your possession at any time. This rule is easy to under-

43

stand and apply for all of us who can count to five, however haltingly.

The next rule, which prescribes minimum size limits for abalone, is much more difficult. The size of an abalone is measured by its greatest shell diameter. The minimum size for red abalone, the most prevalent kind found in Northern California, is seven inches in diameter. We emphasize that you cannot have a red abalone that is "about seven inches" in diameter, or even an abalone that is seven inches in diameter minus a quarter of an inch. The game warden carries a set of calipers with prongs exactly seven inches apart, and if your abalone cannot touch both prongs at once, you pay. A fine of $50 for a 1/8-inch oversight is not uncommon. The minimum size for green, pink, or white abalone is six inches; five inches for black abalone; and four inches for all other species.

Even if you try to comply with these size limits it is often difficult to measure the abalone accurately. One regulation states that any person catching mollusks (abalone) with a size limit must also carry an accurate measuring device. Calipers are the only really accurate device, but most people try to get by with measurement markings on the tool they use to catch the abalone. But be careful with these tools, because almost every abalone appears to be of legal size right after you catch it; this is part optical illusion and part optimism. So play it safe when you catch an abalone of marginal size. Game wardens take no excuses, such as "I measured the abalone for half an hour and really thought it was big enough," or "My iron got bent in the middle and that must have thrown my measurement off." Seriously, a slight mistake, and you pay money. So aim for the really big ones; it makes better sport anyway.

Any abalone that proves to be undersized "must be replaced immediately with the shell outward to the surface of the rock from which detached." Fortunately this rule is as difficult to enforce as it is to comply with. Just put an undersized abalone back on the nearest homey-looking rock.

Next, the tool you use to take abalone must conform to strict specifications. Knives, screwdrivers, and sharp instruments are prohibited. Likewise, gaff hooks and spears are prohibited. (And north of Yankee Point, scuba equipment for abalone catching is illegal.) The tool must be straight or with a curve having a radius of not less than 18 inches. It must be at least 3/4 inches wide, and at least 1/16 inches thick. All edges must be rounded and free of sharp points. These stipulations are imposed because if you pierce an abalone with your tool but do not catch it, or it turns out to be too small, it bleeds to death anyway. Thus, your tool must have no sharp edge. Abalone irons sold commercially are usually legal, although often they are clumsy compared to homemade devices. To start with, you should use either an iron sold in a dive shop or one provided by an experienced diver friend. After you understand how to catch abalone and what is required of the tool, you can make your own.

Finally, one provision states that "all fish, mollusks, crustaceans and amphibia, or any device or apparatus designed to be and capable of being used to take them, and all licenses, must be exhibited on the demand of any authorized officer." The essence of this section is that you are not "safe" once you leave the beach or get to your car. If a game warden thinks you have been fishing, he can ask to see your catch, your equipment, and your license at any time.

The Fish and Game rules should be strictly followed for several reasons. First, they are law, and violations bring stiff penalties. Second, while the edible sea animals are not endangered species, it upsets the ecological balance of an area when one or more species of inhabitants is suddenly cleaned out. Third, it is morally offensive to take more than you need of anything.

Enough preaching. On to the real problem of beach access.

5 GETTING TO THE WATER

The problem of beach access causes outpourings of indignation, outrage, and self-righteousness among all parties concerned. Since only a fraction of California's 1100 mile coastline is publicly owned (and some of this public land is military), the diver who restricts himself to true public access severly limits the number of places he can dive. Further, the state-owned beaches with public access are, not surprisingly, relatively overpopulated and fished out. Also, the state or county tends to acquire the smooth, sandy beaches that are most pleasant for picnicking but least interesting for diving. While you can dive from public beaches, it is only at the cost of several inconveniences.

Where private property intervenes between the nearest road and the beach, the following paradox occurs: While the actual beach (the land below the median high water mark), belongs to the "people of the State of California," there is no statutory provision for an "easement" or a "right of way" to enable any particular person in California to cross the intervening private land from the road to the beach. Thus, the people of the State of California have a right to be on public roads, and a right to be on the beach, but no right to get from one to the other if there is intervening private property. Such is the current state of the law.

Most private property owners take one of three stands toward allowing access across their land to the beach. The first is to implicitly permit access by not posting signs or raising fences. (This is not the usual practice; almost all private land is posted and fenced.) The second practice is to prohibit public use of access paths except on payment of an admission fee, usually between 50 cents and $2 per person. The third stand is to prohibit public access altogether. (Some landowners who prohibit public access make exceptions for people who specifically ask permission to cross and whose looks the landowner likes. However, the most common result of requesting permission to cross from a farmer or landowner is the rather unpleasant directive to get the hell out.)

If you want access through private property, you have to either pay money or take risks. The risks entail being confronted by an angry property owner and told to get off the land. Nothing bad can happen to you legally if you acquiesce, but you do have to retrace your steps with all your gear and then search for another access point. And it is unnerving and disruptive of a pleasant day to be constantly worried about the imminent appearance of an antagonistic property owner. While you are only guilty of a trespass if you fail to leave the property when requested to do so, this legal position is small comfort when the owner is making extravagant threats. For example, we were once run off a diving campsite that was arguably within the highwater boundary of the beach. But the eviction took place at gunpoint, late at night, and we were not about to make a technical legal argument to the vigilante patrol.

To be slightly encouraging, California law is slowly changing to allow greater public access to the beach. For example, Proposition 20, the Coastline

Initiative, was passed in the November 1972 election, and prohibits a city or county from approving a plan for a coastline development unless the plan provides "reasonable public access" to the beach. However, this new law does not affect existing developments, like Sea Ranch in Sonoma County, which in 1969 gained monopoly control of some 14 miles of coast by spending a great deal of money on lawyers and public relations. You can read the lurid details in the Ralph Nader Study Group Report *Politics of Land.* * Nor does Proposition 20 affect the ability of private homeowners to exclude access to the beach. And while the California Supreme Court looks favorably on increased public access, the best that it has actually done for the cause is to state that a path over private land used by the public for more than five years without objection cannot subsequently be closed.

Here are a few things you can do about this state of affairs. First, the people who teach you how to dive can also tell you about certain public beaches that are good for diving, and also about any free private accesses that they know about. Next, you can ask other divers you meet at these beaches where other good locations are. While you can expect that the average diver is withholding information about any "special" spots that he has personally found after arduous and perhaps risky search expeditions, most divers will give you information about places that are well-known for their access.

A third source of information is the game warden. If you see one, try to strike up an amiable conversation and ask whether he knows where access to the beach is permitted. He has no reason to hold back anything, and might pass on a good tip if he likes you. Further, if his recommended location turns out to be guarded by an unsympathetic landowner, you can sometimes lower the level of tension by

mentioning the "authorization" by the game warden.

The most difficult but potentially most rewarding approach is to spend a day cruising the coast road over a stretch where you think the diving conditions should be good. Stop at all the turnouts and look for NO TRESPASSING signs. Because owners who want to prohibit access spare no expense in telling you so, the absence of a new, large sign indicates a good likelihood that you can cross there. Look further for signs of a worn path from the road in the direction of the beach. Drive for a couple of miles in both directions from a potential access point and note whether the land is being actively farmed, or being sparsely grazed with sheep or cattle, or is undeveloped, and where the nearest house or building is. As a group, farmers are the least amenable to people tracking across the fields, with ranchers less hostile, and absentee landlords, by default, the most open to allowing access.

Of course, you can always attempt to find the owner of the land traversed by the potential access path and ask him about his position on the subject. While this often takes time and can be unpleasant, so is being intercepted in midfield and having to trudge back to the car. Finding access through private property is a time-consuming effort fraught with difficulty, but the rewards of finding a special cove not used by the general public are extremely valuable.

We find it very, very offensive to pay money to a surly and antagonistic landowner for the privilege of crossing to land that belongs to the public; therefore, we almost never use private access that requires an admission fee. However, if you can stomach this exploitation, many nice beaches are accessible for a price, particularly on the Sonoma Coast.

*Politics of Land. New York: Grossman Publishers, 1973.

6 WHERE TO DIVE IN NORTHERN AND CENTRAL CALIFORNIA

This chapter discusses dive spots clustered around California's four coastal population centers: the greater San Francisco Bay Area; the central coast from Morro Bay to Santa Barbara, including the Channel Islands; the Los Angeles Area, including Catalina Island; and the San Diego Area. Each of the four sections mentions the best spot in the area to learn and become comfortable with the ocean as well as additional spots recommended for interest and variety

The dive spots mentioned here are our favorites. When we dive, we almost always go to one of them, or we decide to explore and spend the day looking for a hidden cove off the beaten path. Our spots described here will expose you to a variety of underwater settings from which you can develop your personal tastes in diving. Eventually you will find your own favorite places.

NORTHERN CALIFORNIA

Where to learn to dive: Monterey Bay

In Northern California, the first diving spot to become familiar with is the Monterey Bay Area. This is the best place for a beginning diver because it is calm, safe, beautiful, and interesting. You should dive in the bay until you are thoroughly comfortable with the mechanics of diving, and the techniques of swimming around and through kelp, and until you become familiar with the extent of your endurance and your feelings about being out in the ocean. Since Monterey is almost always calm enough to dive safely, you will not in the first few dives have to make crucial judgments about whether the state of the ocean is compatible with your level of competence. Further, since there are

usually great numbers of free and scuba divers at the places we will mention, you will be safe and should feel safe, too.

Don't get the wrong idea, though: Diving in Monterey Bay is *not* the aquatic equivalent of a dry run. On the contrary, the underwater terrain at the places we'll describe is unusually rich in colorful plant and animal sea life. The rocky bottoms are covered with starfish, anemones, and kelp and seaweed of astounding brilliance. Also, the kelp beds at the breakwater particularly are graced with an extravagant congregation of delicious fish. Thus, Monterey Bay is both an ideal place to learn to dive and an exhilarating spot for even the seasoned diver.

We recommend three particular access points, all of which are well known and much frequented by free and scuba divers.

First is the Coast Guard breakwater at the begin-

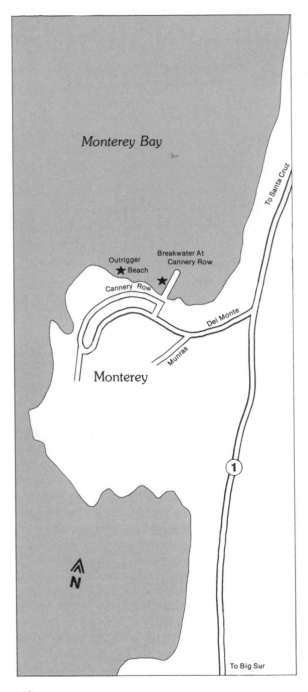

Monterey Bay

To Santa Cruz

Outrigger Beach

Breakwater At Cannery Row

Cannery Row

Del Monte

Munras

Monterey

1

N

To Big Sur

ning of Cannery Row. The rocky bottom on the south side of the breakwater is a haven for seemingly limitless numbers of perch, cod, and other fish. See the map for the precise location (although the breakwater is such a landmark that you can ask anybody for directions). Unfortunately, the divers' regular parking lot at the foot of the breakwater was recently closed off by the owner, making it more difficult to park and get you and your equipment from the car to the water. But at least *you* won't be lugging scuba tanks for a couple of blocks. It is best to park as close as possible to the breakwater, then, depending on your personal preference, put on your wetsuit at the car and walk like a frogman to the beach (in your sneakers, of course, not your flippers), or carry your equipment to the beach and leave your clothes in a pile. Of course, you have to find some place for your car keys where they can't accidentally get lost in the sand.

The first time you dive at the breakwater, you should take a preliminary walk out to the end and observe the terrain. The large rocks visible above the surface next to the breakwater provide the home for fish and the foundation for the kelp. When you dive, you will stay within 30 or 40 feet of the breakwater itself, diving in and out of the rocks and kelp that border it. You will never have to swim far to reach solid ground: This knowledge should provide some psychological security for the first few dives.

When you have gone as far on the breakwater as the public is permitted to go, you will notice that the rest of the structure provides a sunbathing place for great numbers of seals. Depending on how far from shore you swim in the direction of the seals, you are more or less likely to see some of them diving in your vicinity. These are friendly creatures and will not bother you; don't bother them either. In the same area, you might also see what look like tiny seals; these are sea otters. They are

Point Lobos is calm and beautiful – and carefully managed by the State Park authorities.

playful often to the point of teasing. It is not uncommon to see a sea otter swimming langorously on its back, holding a large abalone in its forepaws, and munching on it like a kid with the biggest fudgecicle on the block.

Back at the beach, once you have donned your equipment and your group has checked each other out, make a dive plan, and go in. The first hundred yards or so provide only a sandy bottom without kelp or fish. Thus, you can concentrate on getting warm, on taking practice dives, and on getting coordinated with your group without distractions from underwater. Once you reach the large rocks piled up next to the breakwater and the tall kelp plants afloat on the surface, you can start diving for pleasure. We usually plan to continue swimming out toward the end of the breakwater, diving periodically, until we find a particularly beautiful place or a particularly good fishing ground. Then we tie our float to a branch of kelp so that no one has to tend it, and dive until we feel like moving on. Remember, the closer you get your

facemask to the rocks on the bottom, the more you see. Of course, you can get a spectacular view in the opposite direction, from the bottom looking up through the sunrays and kelp branches to the surface. The kelp leaves provide a roosting place for several types of large and beautiful snails. Also, there are both free-swimming fish and hole-dwellers. The free-swimmers simply travel in schools along the kelp at depths of five to 40 feet. The hole-dwellers live in crevices around the beneath the rocks next to the breakwater. Needless to say, it is more comfortable for the novice to watch and follow the free-swimmers than to poke a nose into holes at the bottom. However, as you get more comfortable with the colors and shapes of underwater life, you will find yourself more curious and less squeamish about delving into recesses where, for example, the big cod live.

We suggest that, when finished diving for the day, you swim back to shore the way you came. You could also climb out on the rocks at the end of the public part of the breakwater and walk back on dry

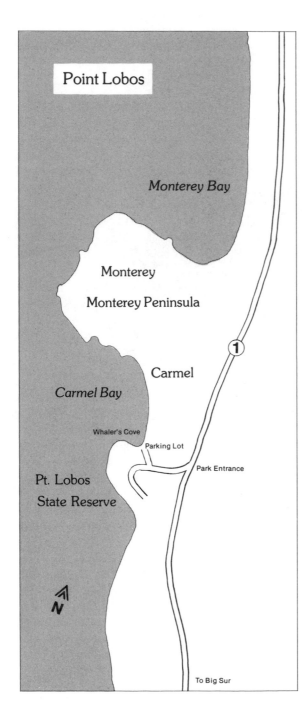

land, but this has two disadvantages. First, as a learner, you should practice gauging your energy so that you have plenty left to navigate back to the beach. It would be a mistake to count on having a place to climb out of the water right next to where your good diving is, because you rarely do. You should let the nearness of the breakwater provide some security for you while learning to dive, but not treat it as a crutch. Second, there are signs on the breakwater prohibiting skindiving off the rocks, so we assume there is a similar prohibition against climbing onto the rocks or breakwater from the ocean. But at times, when we have caught an exceptionally heavy batch of fish and we have landlubber friends on the breakwater to help carry the fish back, we climb out at the end of the public breakwater and walk back.

The second Monterey Bay spot we recommend is the beach to the north of the Outrigger Restaurant, down Cannery Row from the breakwater. This beach is equally calm and probably just as pretty underwater, but the fish don't congregate in such numbers. There is a public parking lot across the street from the beach. Again, the water is almost always calm and there are plenty of other divers in the vicinity. Your best dive plan is to spot patches of kelp from the shore and make for a chosen patch as a group, diving along the way. The diving here is much more open than at the breakwater, because you can go almost anywhere on the horizon you want to dive, rather than being "tied" to the breakwater. Thus the Outrigger beach provides a good place to practice planning an open water dive, searching around for an underwater spot you like, and providing enough time and energy to return to the beach.

Whaler's Cove

A third learning spot is Whaler's Cove in Point Lobos Marine Reserve, south of the Monterey Peninsula. The coastal setting, rocky cliffs topped with cypress groves, certainly beats downtown Monterey for background. The diving is comparable to that in the Bay, and visibility is often better. However, since it is a state marine reserve, diving is carefully regulated as follows. First, only a limited number of divers are permitted at any one time; thus your chances of getting in on summer weekends is low. All divers must sign for a permit at the entrance gate, and are required to have a diving flag and a float, a flotation vest, and except for free divers, a certification card. Finally, no marine life may be taken in the reserve.

Point Lobos is a fine place to learn if you can accommodate yourself to all these regulations. On a weekday in the fall, such an accommodation is well worth it. You can park right at the edge of Whaler's Cove and swim out through the mouth into some of the clearest water on the California coast. Moreover, the reserve itself is laced with carefully marked trails and picnic areas in unique, spectacular scenery.

Half Moon Bay

The area around Half Moon Bay, 20 minutes south of San Francisco, offers the nearest good diving to that city. Our special preference is for the spot bounded by the right angle of the breakwater just west of Princeton-by-the-Sea and the adjacent sandy beach with the ITT-Air Force installation on top of the cliff. The appeal of this spot is its variety of underwater terrain and marine life. At low tide, a flat rocky shelf is uncovered at the north end of the sandy beach, and tidepool watchers arrive in hordes to observe seastars, anemones, and the multifarious other flora and fauna. The partially exposed rocks hide rock crabs that you can catch by hand. When this area is covered at higher tides, you can lure the crabs out by means of the crab lures (See the chapter "What to Catch and How") and then dive for them. Most divers concentrate around the patches of kelp 100 or so yards offshore, within the expanse of the right angle described above. You can enter the water from the breakwater and swim toward a patch of kelp, or you can swim out from the sandy

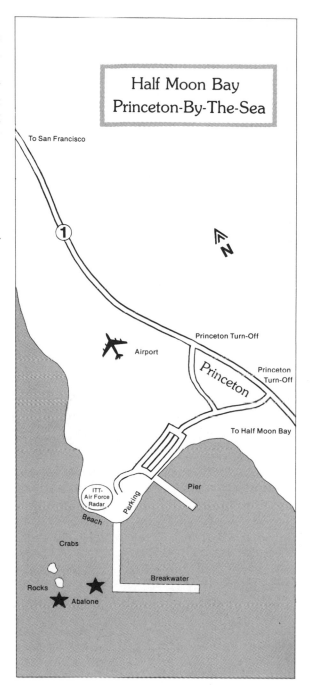

Half Moon Bay
Princeton-By-The-Sea

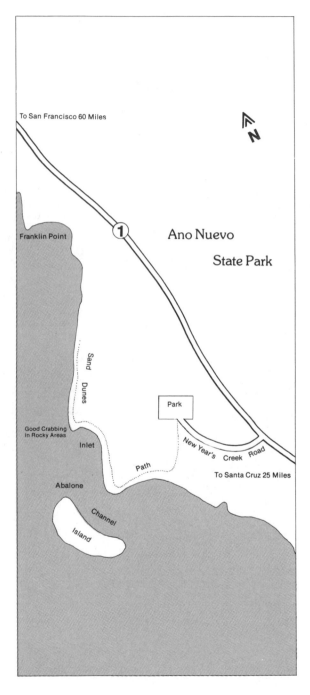

To San Francisco 60 Miles

Franklin Point

Ano Nuevo

State Park

①

Sand Dunes

Park

Good Crabbing
In Rocky Areas

Inlet

New Year's Creek Road

Path

To Santa Cruz 25 Miles

Abalone

Channel

Island

N

beach. When swells can be seen crashing against the breakwater, it is more comfortable to enter from the beach and exit there as well. Offshore, the bottom is flat and rocky, and rather barren. But interspersed with this terrain are bolder rock formations that provide anchorage for the kelp and homes for good-sized abalone and just plain big lingcod and cabezon. The kelp above attracts perch and other free-swimming fish. Also, crabs are often seen and caught as they stroll around in these areas. The secret of diving here is to swim from kelp bed to kelp bed and dive underneath. The kelp leaves floating on the surface act as flags for the good rocky areas and much of the rest of the area is flat and dull.

Usually, the vicinity of the large rocks off the westernmost end of the sandy beach is too rough to dive in, because the northwest swells break over these rocks. (This leaves the areas described above relatively calm. But on the rare, very calm days, the bottom around these rocks is noteworthy for the abalone that sit out in the open on the flat shelves. However, these abalone are rather difficult to see, because the flora and fauna living on their shells provide very good protective coloration. Also, the water is usually somewhat clearer in this rocky area than near the breakwater. You should know that around Half Moon Bay generally, the visibility is often short, say five to 10 feet. Thus, we recommend the area for its tangible rewards of abalone, fish, and crabs, rather than for any underwater aesthetics. Also, the setting is convenient for picnicing; the fishing village of Princeton-by-the-Sea provides a scenic background; and it is very close to the Northern California population centers.

Ano Nuevo State Park

Ano Nuevo is about 60 miles south of San Francisco, on New Year's Creek Road off Route 1. To get to Ano Nuevo you pass many miles of enjoyable but uninspiring diving areas along the San Mateo County coastline. If you don't mind the additional driving time, try Ano Nuevo. It's a perfectly fine place to dive, and is graced with other exceptional qualities as well: large expanses of sand dunes to wander and play in; a terrain that varies from stark cliffs to long stretches of sandy beach; and marine life that includes not only abalone but also rock crabs and many varieties of clams and cockles. Thus, Ano Nuevo is an ideal place for an outing, with opportunities for picnicking, biking, sunbathing, crabbing, clam-digging, and any other activities that a lovely coastal setting inspires you to pursue.

Ano Nuevo has two characteristics that require advance planning on your part. First, it has become quite popular, so park rangers now control the number of people in the park at any time. While this measure is a worthwhile effort to keep crowds from destroying flora and fauna, it also means that you should plan your expedition to arrive there in early morning to avoid a disappointing wait. The second drawback is that the park rangers, purportedly to protect the resident rabbits and deer, stringently enforce a rule prohibiting dogs in the entire park area.

When you arrive at Ano Nuevo (see map), you should have all of your equipment and supplies fairly efficiently packed, preferably in backpacks, because it is a good hike from the parking areas to the beach. Luckily, it is also one of the most lovely coastal hikes we have seen, across flowered fields with rolling hills in the background. Follow the well-worn path until you come to the sand dunes, and then either walk over the dunes within sight of the water on your left, or climb down and walk on the beach itself. At low tide, the beach is well exposed. Walk until you reach the point of land across from the island with the abandoned Coast Guard station. This is where you and your friends should stop and confer about the state of the ocean, wind, and weather, and your plans for diving and whatever else.

Standing on the point facing the island, you notice that a small, sheltered inlet cuts back into the land to your right. At the far northern end of the inlet is another small point, and beyond is a great stretch of open sandy beach. You can always find a spot protected from the wind on one or the other side of this northern point.

The best diving at Ano Nuevo is in the channel between island and shore. Abalone live on smaller rocks in the channel, but the greatest concentrations of abalone are found farther out, beyond the inlet proper. Thus, you can dive either from the first point you come to, directly across from the island, or walk around the cove and head out from any point on the beach. We usually walk about three-quarters of the way around the cove and settle in, because this is also the best place to find crabs. Depending on how much equipment you are carrying and how much isolation you are interested in, you can park yourselves right there on the point or head around the cove as far as you wish.

Diving at Ano Nuevo can be tricky when the tide is going out and the water is rough, because very strong seaward currents are created in the funnel between the land point and the island. You should not take your first open ocean dive at Ano Nuevo unless you stay clearly in the cove and away from the island channel. Even if you have dived several times in open water and feel fairly competent, we strongly suggest that the first time you dive at Ano Nuevo you include in your party an experienced diver who knows the area well. (If nothing else, an experienced person will lead you to the abalone more directly.)

If you are a person of faith, there is an interesting way to find the abalone in the south part of the Ano Nuevo channel (this method is applicable in other areas of similar marine geography). Abalone can live only on rocks. The south part of the channel is mostly sand with large patches of rocks here and there. Fine sand is white and the rocks are dark; you swim slowly on the surface staring directly below yourself, and any dark spot you perceive, however dimly, is a patch of rocks that will be inhabited by lots of abalone (since they experience a housing crisis in this mostly sandy environment). This ap-

Jenner-Russian Gulch cove embodies the spirit of the rugged north coast. Abalones like it too.

proach works fine, even on days when the water is troubled, because only a very slight change in the hue of the bottom is needed to call your attention, *if you have faith.*

If you are interested in crabs, then make sure your day at Ano Nuevo includes a low tide. During a minus tide of any size, you will see at the north end of the cove and continuing up the coast, uncovered shelves of rock lined with horizontal crevices. When the tide goes out, the rock crabs stay in these crevices and in those under the rock shelves. You simply approach an uncovered stretch of rock and look in the crevices or feel under those that are still covered with water. These rock crabs are very docile and very lethargic when resting in these cracks. Don't worry that they'll pinch you, because they rest with their large pincers tucked under their arms, so to speak, and are thus unlikely to pinch a hand that grabs them. Also, there are no other sea animals living in these cracks that might bother you,

so be intrepid. When you see a crab exposed in a crevice, or feel one under a rock in a little water, grab it by whatever you can and yank it out and toss it into the open. Then, carefully pick it up from behind and put it in your sack. Move along the crevices carefully — where you find one crab you will find several.

Sand cockling is equally easy. Just bring a pointed shovel and dig out scoops of rock, sand, and mud in areas exposed at low tide. Choose a place that is equal parts of small stones and sand. Usually, residual water fills up your holes as you dig, but when you overturn a sand cockle you will see it. A healthy sand cockle will be shut tight. In any case, there are enough other sand cocklers at Ano Nuevo at low tide for you to learn from.

Unfortunately, there is no overnight camping at Ano Nuevo, but it is an easy day trip from anywhere in the San Francisco Bay Area.

54

Jenner-Russian Gulch

The town of Jenner marks the beginning of the rugged north coast where big abalone thrive. Just four miles north of Jenner is a cove that is very special to us; the scene of many wonderful dives, beach barbecues and magnificent sunsets. The access paths cross land that is currently privately owned, although the County of Sonoma recently attempted to purchase the area, and the State is also interested in acquiring it for public recreation. The spot is beautiful and always worth a visit, whether to dive, to watch the sun go down, to socialize, or to mend one's city-battered spirit. We divulge its location with the hope that it will be shared by many but not destroyed by people pollution.

The cove is reached in two stages: First, by getting yourself to Jenner. We recommend Route 101 north and then any of the roads that cross west to meet Route 116. Turn north on Route 1 for four miles until you arrive at Russian Gulch, where the road crosses a riverbed that is usually dry. You can park on the side of the road and follow the riverbed out until you see the wide, sandy ocean outlet. Then turn up the slope to the north, cross the meadow, and descend the winding path on the far side of the huge rock point. The path is well-worn but steep, and is often muddy during winter. The cove beach is rocky and completely covered with driftwood. You can dive right there in the cove, or at the end of the beach past the two monumental rocks. Often it is too rough to dive here; the rolling swells from the northwest roll onto the beach and into the cove. The sight is spectacular but incompatible with diving. If it is calm enough to dive, you will find abalone everywhere. We suggest restraint in taking abalone out of the cove itself; the biggest ones are outside the cove around the large rocks.

Also, there are rich mussel beds on the surf-swept rocks here. Sand cockles live in the rocky-sandy areas exposed at low tides. We even caught an octopus here that had failed to move into deeper water at one of the very low tides.

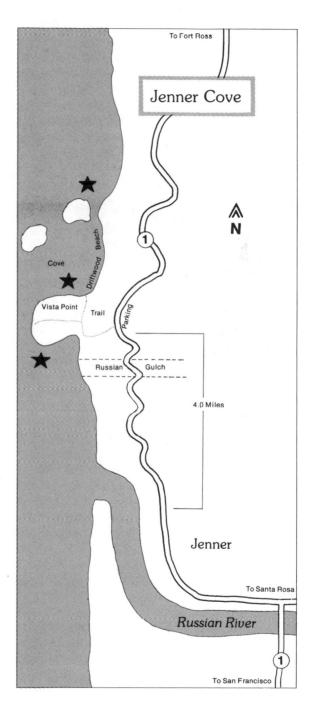

55

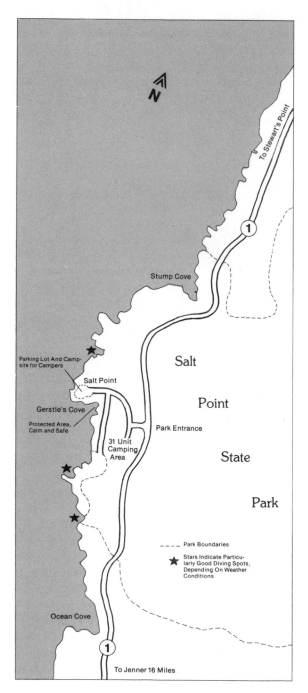

With the fairly long hike from car to beach, visiting the cove requires a long day's trip from the Bay Area. Driving from San Francisco takes about two hours.

Salt Point State Park

Salt point is very close to paradise, and just 125 miles north of San Francisco. The rugged, rocky coastal cliffs are strikingly handsome; the pine forests in the inland hills are lovely; and the diving is very, very good. For several reasons, we recommend weekend camping at Salt Point as your introduction to abalone diving. First, even if the ocean turns out to be too rough to dive, you cannot help but have an exhilerating time hiking and sightseeing. Second, Gerstle's Cove (see map) is a marine reserve protected both from rough ocean and from abalone hunting divers. We suggest that you dive first in Gerstle's Cove to acquaint yourself with "abalone country." While you are not permitted to catch abalone or any other sea creature in the reserve, you can get a good look at them in their habitat. And since the cove is sheltered from much of the coastal surf action, you can take a practice or reconnaissance dive in its calm waters if you have doubts about your competency in the adjacent more exposed areas. Third, there are good numbers of abalone in the coves and open ocean throughout the park, so that your chances of catching some are high.

During the summer, the Salt Point campground is packed, as are all of California's overburdened coastal resources. (This unfortunate jam-up is caused by the fact that of the 1100 miles of California coastline, a mere fraction is available for public use.) If you have a camper, you can park out on the end of Salt Point itself. This area is exposed and often windy, but spectacularly beautiful. If you are camping with a tent, you must camp up in the forested campground (see map). The campsites are allocated first-come, first-served and you have little chance of finding a place by arriving on a summer weekend. Before you set out, you can call the ranger to find out how crowded the place is and what your chances are of getting a space. The rangers are extremely friendly and helpful.

We strongly suggest that you visit Salt Point during the fall, anytime between Labor Day and Thanksgiving. The hordes of vacationers have returned to their workaday worlds and the California Indian summer keeps the days warm and takes the chill out of the evenings. But most important, the ocean is in relative repose, so the diving will be easy-going and the visibility will be at its best.

In choosing a particular place to dive at Salt Point, you will find yourself embarrassed by riches. Each cove has its particular charm, and each section of adjacent cliffs has unique rock formations. Basically, you have three choices. First, you can drive down to the end of Salt Point itself and dive straight out into the open ocean. This has the advantage of being simple and direct, but for obvious reasons the water is often the roughest off the point. We prefer finding a cove.

You can park on the point and hike north, either wearing or carrying your wetsuit. The first cove you come to is a good one. The path from the parking lot takes you to the rocky beach where you dive from. Notice that the whole area is covered with rocks of different sizes and shapes. This is the best indicator of abalone territory. However, you cannot saunter into the water here as at Monterey, for there's no gradual sandy beach. Instead, you have to clamber over rocks, often covered with slippery seaweed, until you get into water deep enough (two to three feet) to launch yourself. Even then you will run into rocks while you half swim and half crawl for deeper water. Since you will feel as awkward and clumsy as a drunken seal on ice skates the first couple of times you try such an entrance, it is extremely important to make these initial attempts only in very calm water (as decided by your teacher-friend's good

judgment), because the last problem you need is some surf knocking you around.

Planning your first couple of dives, whether at this particular cove or at any other, you might try to go in at midtide, halfway between low and high tide. This has two advantages: You don't have to struggle over all the rocks that would be exposed at dead low tide, nor do you have to dive as deep to reach bottom as you would at high tide.

If you dive in this first cove north of the point, you should not plan to swim out past the mouth of the cove on your first couple of dives. The open ocean off Salt Point has quite a bit of current and drift, as well as the roughest water. There are lots of abalone in the cove itself, so swim out until you reach a kelp patch where the water is deep enough to dive comfortably in (seven feet or more). Follow a kelp stalk down to the very bottom, grab onto the stem of the kelp to hold yourself stationary, and look very carefully at the rock the kelp is attached to. Look under the rock, and in the vicinity. Shortly, you will find yourself an abalone. Upon such a sighting, you of course deftly insert your abalone iron between the abalone shell and the rock it's attached to, flick it off and grab it with your free hand. Return to the surface and measure your catch to see if it is legal size.

We must prepare you for the unfortunate likelihood that you will not deftly snatch the first abalone you see from its rock and into your hand. Catching an abalone takes some skill. When you see your first one, most probably you will be so unsure that it actually is an abalone that you will run out of air and be forced to return to the surface before you can take any affirmative action. No trouble, however; where there is one abalone there is a batch of them. Dive again in the same place, using the same search technique, holding onto a kelp stalk and peering keenly under all rocks and into all crevices. The next abalone you see will move you to action. However, hand-eye coordination is somewhat different underwater, and your attempt to scoop your prey off the rock will very likely be unsuccessful. You will

57

probably hit the rock the abalone is attached to or bang the abalone on its shell. In either case, the abalone will realize that trouble is at hand, and will hold onto the rock with great tenacity. Once you scare an abalone by an unsuccessful attack, you should look for another and catch it unaware; a frightened one is too difficult for a beginner to pry off.

When diving on the open coast, you should keep a close watch on changing conditions of the ocean. A rising wind can quickly stir up troublesome surf. If you are diving in the middle of the cove and you notice the water getting rougher and waves breaking over the rocks where you entered the water, you should hold a conference about getting out earlier than you had planned. If getting into the water over rocks is awkward, getting out is worse because you are tired and wet. And you can get knocked about by surf just as much while getting out as while getting in. Thus, it pays to keep a sharp eye out for changes in the ocean along the open coast. Wait for a set of big waves to break, and then swim in through the smaller ones.

Other Salt Point diving spots are south of South Cove. The cove itself is rather picked over, leaving the abalone few and far between. However, since there are plenty of big abalones only a couple of hundred yards south of the parking lot, you can park and hike from there. Any place south of South Cove will afford good diving. We like the little inlet marked on the map simply for diving, and the cove at the end of the park path for picnicking as well. Choose your own spots according to the relative calmness of the water, accessibility of a beach where you can get in, and the availability of other exits in case you drift some. We recommend that you stay in a cove, and return to the beach you started from, at least until you are rather familiar with this open ocean diving.

A final tip for your first couple of abalone dives at Salt Point: If for some reason the water there is a little too rough for you, or the rocks make you particularly nervous, but you really want to try to catch an abalone, drive south a few miles to Stillwater Cove. This spot has a calm, sandy beach offering easier access to the water. The disadvantages are that the visibility is worse precisely because of the sand in the water, and the abalone are scarcer. However, it is a good place to try serious abalone diving if Salt Point is a little too rough and you are tired of sightseeing in Gerstle's Cove.

Almost all of the Sonoma County coast north of Jenner provides wonderful abalone diving. The only two problems are finding public access to the beach and finding calm enough waters to enter and exit. The coves at Salt Point are particularly good, but you should stop wherever your fancy is caught and check the place out. Remember the tactics described in Chapter 5 for avoiding problems of trespassing.

CENTRAL CALIFORNIA: MORRO BAY TO SANTA BARBARA

In this hundred-odd mile stretch of coast there are two distinct population centers and dive areas. They share the trait of generally short visibility, say five to 15 feet. Thus, divers in this area must continually choose between diving locally or taking a moderate to long trip either north (to Monterey), south (to San Diego), or west (to the island diving at Santa Cruz, Anacapa, or Santa Rosa). The choice is a real one, we assure you, because local diving is thoroughly enjoyable in itself, and the countryside and coastal settings are particularly appealing.

Where to Learn to Dive: Morro Bay

Morro Bay has two striking landmarks — Morro Rock itself and the three industrial chimneys at the foot of the bay. Morro Bay comes very close to providing good, all-weather diving, because the Rock forms a natural harbor that is further protected by a manmade jetty of impressive proportions. The good diving, then, is inside the breakwater but out

Dive in the channel at Morro Bay. The rock (left) and the chimneys are reliable landmarks.

of the boat channel. You can park next to the dive spots if you follow the road to the rock and continue past the unimproved parking areas until you round a bend and see the foot of the breakwater about 200 yards away. Your learning dives can be made either in the kelp beds on the edge of the channel (pictured below) or off the sheltered side of the breakwater. Both spots are calm and safe for learning, and, further, each has a different terrain and harbors different marine life.

The bottom at the edge of the channel is clean except for a few old tires. The rocks on the bottom are covered with scallops. Though these tend to be small, their numbers compensate if you are thinking about a scallop dinner. We suspect, though we can't prove it, that the abundance of scallops in this unexpected spot may be related to warm water effluent from the nearby PG&E plant. This effluent does *not* involve organic or chemical pollution, as is proven by the large number of good-size market

crabs, particularly in the spring. By and large, the channel at Morro Bay offers both scallops and crabs that are the easiest to take in all our experience. It also has some small lingcods.

Having taken your fill of *hors d'oeuvre*, you might consider walking to the breakwater road for a fish course. Depending on the tide, the area right next to the breakwater and the end of the road might have anywhere from one foot to three feet of water. You can either walk or swim to the end of the breakwater. If you swim, you will be able to pick up hundreds of cone-like, delicately colored shells that would make a wonderful necklace.

On the landside toward the end of the breakwater, in the protected area that is always fit for diving, the water reaches 10 to 15 feet or more, depending on the tide. The blocks of the breakwater itself shelter very big lingcods and quantities of perch. Rumor has it that the ocean side of the breakwater, which can be dived in only in calm weather, has

59

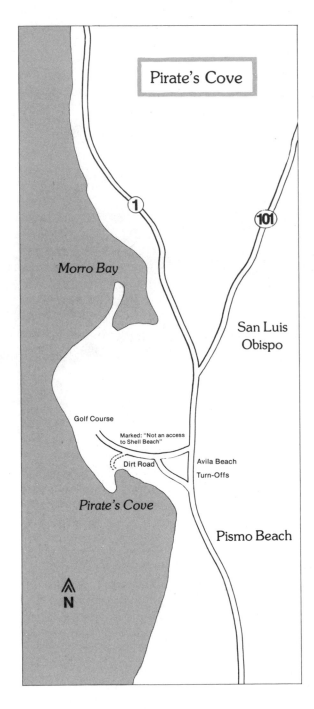

Pirate's Cove

Morro Bay

San Luis
Obispo

Golf Course

Marked: "Not an access
to Shell Beach"

Dirt Road

Avila Beach
Turn-Offs

Pirate's Cove

Pismo Beach

N

even bigger lingcods. We have never tried to verify
that rumor, but there's no reason why it shouldn't
be true, even though most fishermen lie through
their teeth. The sandy area at the very end of the
breakwater is said to have halibut in the summer.
We have never seen any, but halibut are fairly
difficult to find, and we may not have dived there
enough to find them. The terrain certainly looks like
good halibut ground, though.

Pirate's Cove

Among the several fine dive spots in the area from
Morro Bay through San Luis Obispo to Pismo
Beach, Pirate's Cove is not exceptional for its diving
but for its coastal setting. Remember that the underwater visibility on this part of the coast is usually
five to 15 feet, and you might want sometimes to
treat yourself to the consolations of fine landscape.
To find Pirate's Cove, take the Avila exit off Route
101 and follow the road until you round a corner and
see a golf course on your left and petroleum company storage tanks on the top of the hill in front of
you. Immediately, you will find an unmarked left
turn up an incline. About halfway up the hill is a sign
saying "This is not an access to Shell Beach." When
you come to a very disreputable dirt parking area
sloping down to your right, *carefully* turn in and
park as close to the cliff as possible.

You can dive either along the rocky coast to the
northwest (on your right as you face the ocean), or
off the rocky point to the southeast (on your left)
after traversing the wide sandy beach. The rocky
area to the north is closer but attracts more divers;
the point south has fewer divers but lots of nudists,
as the sandy beach is a de facto nudist reserve. Not
that this is a disadvantage — there is no reason why
divers and nudists cannot coexist amicably, or even
intermingle. And there is the advantage of being
able to change in and out of your wetsuit without
having to worry about offending the public morality

Looking south from the point at Pirate's Cove across the sandy beach.

Looking north from the Pirate's Cove point after an evening dive.

— or, more to the point, a peace officer. Further, nondivers in your company can swim comfortably off the sandy beach, at least in the summer months.

The bottom consists of good-size rocks intermingled with sandy areas, and the diving is best in the kelp around the rocks. However, during the summer months, the kelp off the southern point blooms very thick, and you should think about skirting it to get to a selected dive spot. Otherwise, you have to crawl over it, which we have honestly described as a tedious and not particularly entertaining mode of transportation.

The waters seem quite full of fish, and the frothy areas behind rocks washed by swells attract good-size perch. The rocks on the bottom also support large numbers of sea urchins, and we suggest you try developing a taste for sea urchin eggs (the poor man's caviar) if you are looking to the ocean for food in this area. Let's face it — abalone are scarce along this part of the coast: Commercial abalone fishing has devastated most of the colonies; scuba divers have picked over the remains; and sea otters are ably scavenging for themselves. Thus, the free diver on the central coast must rely on perserverance to track down abalone in the cracks and crevices where scuba divers are unable to reach. The abalone are there, though sparse.

One compensation for this abalone scarcity is the Pismo clams along the sandy stretches of beaches in Santa Cruz, Monterey, and San Luis Obispo counties. To catch these, dive in fairly shallow water (5 to 10 feet) and poke the sandy bottom with a garden trowel or other handy digging instrument. If you hit something, chances are very good that it is a Pismo clam buried a couple of inches under the sand. In San Luis Obispo County, Pismo clams may be taken at any time of the year, as long as they are over the 4½ inch minimum size. Note, however, that portions of Pismo-Oceano Beach, Morro Beach, and Cayucos Beach have been officially declared "clam preserves" and are off-limits indefinitely. Check section 27.20 of the Fish and Game Regulations for the exact boundaries before diving in.

Santa Barbara

The coast diving in the Santa Barbara area is fun, but the visibility is usually short. Thus, you will probably pick your spots according to the criteria of scenery, accessibility, and other surface considerations. However, Santa Barbara is also the departure point for dive boats going to the clear waters around Santa Cruz, Anacapa, and Santa Rosa Islands. All the considerations we mention in regard to dive trips to Catalina Island (see Los Angeles Area Dive Spots) apply here: You have to weigh the costs of transportation against the benefits of beautiful clearwater diving. Incidentally, the popular consensus is that the Santa Barbara Islands are less "fished over" than Catalina.

If you want to try an island dive, the arrangements are best made through a dive shop. The boats are packed on weekends during the early part of lobster season, which opens the first Wednesday in October, so either get your space early or go during the week. The cost of a day trip is $15 to $18. Be sure to press your agent at the dive shop for his best reports and predictions about ocean conditions before putting your money down. Again, the fall is the best season for clear, calm water.

Anacapa Island

Anacapa is part of the Channel Islands National Monument, and is the island whose waters we frequent. Of the Channel Islands, the sheltered (east) side of Anacapa usually provides the overall best bet for clear water and a calm anchorage.

The bottom is flat with mixed sand and rocks. The larger outcroppings of rock usually have sea urchins on the exposed surfaces and lobsters tucked in underneath. There is plenty of giant kelp attached to the rocks at the bottom, but rather little of the colorful algae covering the rocks themselves. Fish are so plentiful, particularly the golden garibaldi, California's state fish, that they will congregate and eat sea urchin eggs out of your hand. In fact, if you open an urchin underwater with your abalone iron (either cracking it as it sits on the rock, or picking it

This sheltered area on the east side of Anacapa Island is the home of orange Garibaldis.

up and inserting the iron through the foot area underneath) the fish will come in such numbers and stir up so much sand that you will eventually want to move on to clearer water.

We have not seen any of the large red abalone around Anacapa, either on the protected east side or on the more exposed west end. There are patches of green and pink ones, so make sure your iron is calibrated for both the seven inch red abalone minimum and the six inch pink and green minimum.

The area around the natural arch at the southern end of Anacapa has more abalone than elsewhere, probably because there is more surf and fewer divers than in calmer waters.

Caches of abalone left underwater for any period of time, in a submerged goody bag for example, tend to attract rays of different types whose intention is to feed on your abalone. We were shown the appropriate countermeasures by Jim Finch, a professional abalone diver from Santa Barbara, when a bat ray attempted to munch a batch of abalone which we were photographing. Jim's technique was to give the ray a couple of sharp slaps on its rump (or equivalent) with his abalone iron, much as you

might give your cocker spaniel if it shows too much interest in hamburgers on the barbecue.

Big, juicy delicious scallops are also found in rocky crevices around the island. They really are quite difficult to spot because their shells have the rough and irregular surface features of the rocks they are attached to. However, if you are being properly curious and poking into nooks and crannies, you will periodically realize that you are looking at a scallop. Remember, if you are not sure whether it's a rock or a scallop, pry it out with your iron. We've caught plenty of rocks in our time and don't feel embarrassed in the slightest.

Diving at Anacapa or any of the other channel islands involves the excitement of a boat ride and enticement of clearer water than you can find on the mainland coast. To enjoy these two advantages to their fullest, make sure that reports of weather conditions and underwater conditions are favorable before plunking your money down and heading out. It is an exhilarating feeling to dive all day, then with the sun going down behind you, to skim back across the channel, tired yet excited. It is an entirely different feeling to muck around in dirty water, and then to fight your way back to shore through cold evening winds and a bone-rattling chop.

7 WHERE TO DIVE IN SOUTHERN CALIFORNIA

What Monterey Bay is to the Northern California diver, La Jolla is to Southern California brethren. It is beautiful, rich in sea life, and more often calm than not. In addition, the La Jolla shoreline offers the warmest and clearest water anywhere on the West Coast. We will examine several of the best diving spots in the area when we discuss San Diego dive spots below.

The famous La Jolla Cove is the natural place for all Southern Californians to begin diving. We strongly suggest that Los Angeles folk make the easy day trip to La Jolla Cove for their first few dives, because it is usually calmer, safer, and more easily enjoyable for a neophyte than are the dive spots around Los Angeles proper. For example, many Los Angeles dive shop classes take their students to White Point on the Palos Verdes peninsula (see the Los Angeles dive spots below) for their first ocean dive. But La Jolla Cove is calmer, clearer, and more enjoyable than those spots, and we think it very important that you get some sheer pleasure out of your first few dives, to encourage and entice you to learn and practice the fundamental skills. The beauty of the La Jolla Cove and the adjacent marine park is just what you need to instill a carnal desire to dive, even while you are unsure and tentative about the mechanics of diving.

If you live in San Diego, just count your blessings that you have such a chosen spot in your neighborhood. Don't let the fact that it is a tourist attraction stop you. Aside from the fact that you might not be able to park right next to the cove, it will affect little or not at all the pleasure you will get from diving there.

The cove is located about five minutes from downtown La Jolla and is marked by signs. The innermost part of the cove, which faces north, is occupied by an exceedingly small, and usually overcrowded, sandy beach. Most days, a lifeguard is on duty. Above the beach is a very large lawn where people throw Frisbees and picnic. There is also a free public toilet with a fresh-water shower and a senior citizen club with croquet grounds. The beach ends on the seaward side with a minuscule rocky point that bears a commemorative marker of some kind. This point is a good place to enter the water if you want to avoid wading through the children who swarm on the beach itself.

Keep your eyes peeled as you enter: Believe it or not, the marine bottom right next to that point is teeming with lobsters. Local divers don't seem to know this. Each of them probably assumes that the others have been scouring this obvious spot for 30 years but no one seems to have.

A good way to use the La Jolla cove for early training is to enter the water at the rocky point and swim slowly toward the sandy part of the beach, which is an easy exit. Do it several times.

When you return to La Jolla Cove for spearfishing and lobster hunting, the lifeguards require you to enter the water from the rocky steps below the commemorative placque because no spearing devices are permitted in the sandy cove where the swimmers are. Nor are they permitted in the un-

La Jolla Cove is one of the most exhilarating places to dive: it's calm, safe, and quite beautiful.

derwater park. The lifeguard can point out for you the boundaries of the park.

Where to Dive in the Los Angeles Area

For a one-day diving trip in the Los Angeles area, we recommend the Palos Verdes peninsula because it offers a choice of dive spots within 10 or 15 miles of each other, all set in a coastline of magnificent sheer cliffs into which wide coves have been scalloped. Also, each of the four places we will describe has a different exposure to wind and ocean, so you are likely to find at least one area suitable for diving under most weather conditions.

One note of caution: While these coastal cliffs provide a breathtaking backdrop for diving or any other activity you fancy, in their natural state they are very sheer, crumbly, and dangerous to climb. The four places we describe are noteworthy for their safe access from road to beach. If you stick to them, you are not likely to need a Coast Guard helicopter to pick you out of some overgrown sand dune you tumbled into. We mention the problem of access because you will see many footworn paths appearing to lead between cliff top and beach. Please don't mistake the traces of other people's foolhardiness for evidence of a tried-and-true path. The nearby photo shows the top of a "trail" leading down a sheer 200 feet to the beach just north of Rocky Point. The "trail" is well-worn, but extremely dangerous. At Rocky Point, stick to the safe access south of the point, which is described and illustrated below. And at all diving spots, remember that the price exacted for this spectacular coastal setting is simply the exercise of common sense and care in traversing the scenery.

Malaga Cove

Malaga Cove is the first dive spot as you head south from downtown Los Angeles. To reach it, go south on Palos Verdes Boulevard past the Redondo Beach city limits. After you pass Malaga Cove Plaza on your left, take the next right turn onto Via Corta; this winds down to a playing field and an intersection with the Malaga Cove School on your right. Turn right, onto Via Arroyo, proceed to the stop sign, and park in the public lot on your right. To orient yourself, look for a gazebo overlooking the beach. Below and to the left is a swimming club with an outdoor pool, and to the right is the paved access road to the beach (closed to vehicular traffic). Once on the beach at the bottom of the access road, you will notice a clear demarcation between the rocky diving areas to the left and the sandy surfing areas to the right: Diving and surfing areas do not overlap, so there are no runaway surfboard hazards.

When you turn left at the bottom of the access road, you can see a spit of land a couple of hundred yards down the beach, with a tall structure at its seamost point. The Malaga Cove diving area extends from where you are standing to the spit, and as far oceanward as you care to go. At middle-tides, in the approximate center of this rectangle, you can see two solid points protruding above the water. These are the ends of a large, broken down structure of pipes that form an artificial reef and attract fish.

With these landmarks in view, you can walk down the road toward the spit of land until you come to a dead end, make a niche for yourself on the rocky beach, and try the water.

As you swim out, perhaps toward the exposed pipes, the bottom is covered with undulating green eel grass. Often you will come upon what looks like a solid wall of fish — a thick school of small, glittering smelt. This wall melts away from you as you swim through, although no particular fish seems to move.

The steel structure provides shelter for many fish, particularly the golden garibaldi, which is completely protected from spearfishing by the Fish and Game laws. This is a good thing, because the garibaldi is extremely visible and darts for cover only after a diver has entered spearing range. Watch these belated retreats carefully — they often lead directly into lobster holes.

Many other kinds of fish live around the artificial reef, so it is a good place to examine. But remember that when you dive in the vicinity of man-made structures with overhanging pipes or beams, you have to be particularly careful to watch where you are going. You can't assume there is open water above you when you decide to surface. There is a great temptation to continue watching the meanderings of an eye-catching fish while you are surfacing. This temptation must be resisted in favor of protecting your head. Also, around any metal structure, watch out for sharp projections. A little farther out to sea, there are good patches of kelp, bigger fish, and lots of black sea urchins. Less visible but nonetheless available are abalone and lobsters in their holes. Remember that as a free diver you have access to nooks and crannies out of bounds to the equipment-laden scuba diver.

When you head back for shore, carried along by incoming swells, you are likely to discover a slight nuisance when you reach very shallow water, because the bottom consists of uneven small rocks. It is equally awkward to try to walk or crawl over them, particularly because the rocks have barnacle colonies on them which can scratch your bare hands. Since this is a minor irritation and one with no remedy, we mention it only to commiserate.

Rocky Point

Rocky Point, about three miles south of Malaga Cove off Palos Verdes Boulevard, shelters a spectacularly beautiful cove. Turn west off Palos Verdes onto Paseo Lunado, continue past Via Anacapa and past the open field on your left, until the road curves to the right and runs parallel to the cliffs. Here is the

Malaga Cove is naturally separated into the rocky diving area (foreground) and the sunbathing-surfing area.

The best access path to the Rocky Point diving area starts along the storm fencing.

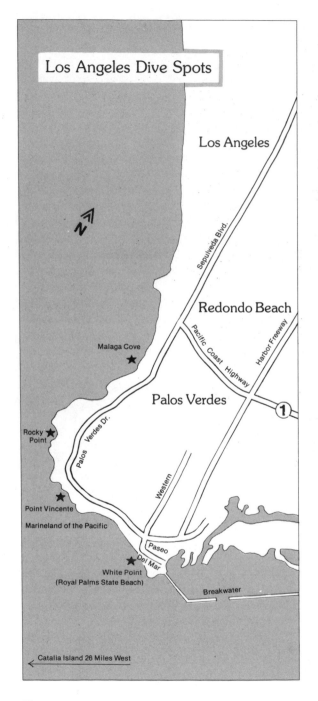

best place for divers to congregate and take a good look at the condition of the ocean. Rocky Point itself is the jut of land to your right. Just out of view around the point is the wreck of the Dominator, now only great chunks of rusting metal strewn around the beach.

If you decide to dive there, you can drive to the access path by turning around and following Paseo del Mar back to Via Anacapa. Two quick right turns put you back on Paseo del Mar with the field on your right, and a school, then Via Alvarado, then residential homes, on your left. Once you have approached the first house on your right; park your car on the side of the road.

For its first 40 feet or so, the access path runs along the storm fence surrounding the yard of the house. The path then winds down to the beach.

There are several places to dive within the cove as well as around Rocky Point past the Dominator. In the center of the cove, relatively close to shore, is a large rock formation. Some of the cove has a sandy bottom, however, and is barren of fish and kelp.

To reach the other spots, you can either swim out and around the point or walk around on the beach and swim out from any point you wish. If you swim northwest or walk along the shore toward Rocky Point, the bottom consists of terraced rocks with not much kelp attached, but covered with small abalone and light blue sea urchins. The abalone are probably too small to catch legally, but this area affords an unusual opportunity to see colonies of abalone on thoroughly exposed surfaces.

Farther northwest, off Rocky Point itself, the terrain is of larger rocks and ledges, different varieties of kelp, and many more fish. The area north of Rocky Point has a consistently rocky bottom and good diving.

The wreck of the Dominator is situated right on the point itself, and if the ocean is at all rough or surging, we avoid approaching the rocks and the

Emerald Bay is one of the popular dive spots around Catalina Island – perhaps too popular, but beautiful nonetheless.

wreck. The rocks and waves that caused the demise of the Dominator could toss a careless diver around to his discomfort.

One dive plan particularly suited to Rocky Point is to swim out from the middle of the cove and dive your way past the abalone ledges, around Rocky Point (staying seaward of any surf action), and as far up the rocky shore as your energy and interest lead you. Then land on the beach and walk back along the shore to your starting point in the cove. This return walk is recommended only if you carry a pair of sneakers in your catch bag, because the path consists entirely of rocks. Also, be sure that your return walk will not coincide with the high water of the day.

The cove beach is a beautiful place for a picnic or fish fry, but you will probably have to bring charcoal with you as there is too little wood on the beach for such fires. Finally, after you make several trips to Rocky Point or a similar cliff-protected cove, you will develop personal preferences for how much food, drink, and other equipment you want to carry down and back out again.

Point Vincente

The Point Vincente area is another spectacular cove surrounded by sheer cliffs, and in addition is graced by a veritable freeway of an access route, labeled a "fishing access" by the government body responsible. The parking lot is right off the highway, and the access path starts well to the right, past the public bathrooms. The cove is rocky and kelp-filled, very similar to the Rocky Point area, except that the Point Vincente cove faces south rather than west. Again, it is probably a good idea to bring a picnic with the intention of settling in for the day, or at least the afternoon, to make the long walk down and back worthwhile.

69

Between Point Vincente and White Point to the south is Marineland, with additional diving areas for you to explore after you have become acquainted with the area.

White Point

To reach White Point (Royal Palms State Beach), continue south on Palos Verdes Boulevard. Turn right on Western Avenue, and proceed downhill. Pass by the first road on the right, and take the second right, a descending switchback. This is the access road.

This unmarked state beach is somewhat different from the three dive spots mentioned above. First, the access road (which although unmarked is easy to find) permits vehicles to drive right down to the ocean. But while there is no cliff-climbing, neither is there the spectacular scenery. Also, the ease of auto access and the southern exposure have made White Point a favorite place for dive shop scuba classes to use for their open water practice dives. The parking lots are often full of visitors of one type or another.

Because White Point is the southernmost dive spot on the Palos Verdes peninsula and has southern exposure, it is more likely to be good compromise dive spot, a place where you can usually get in the water without much effort and enjoy a pleasant dive. While we personally would wind up diving here only if all of the three spots mentioned above had some strike against them on a particular day, we regard White Point as a very welcome safety valve for an easy dive in the Los Angeles area.

When you have reached the parking lots at the beach, you can either turn left toward White Point itself, or go right toward the picnic area. The diving is about the same everywhere along the beach. The bottom is rocky, and there is quite a bit of kelp and fish. You can swim out from anywhere and cruise the length of the beach from White Point to the picnic area.

In sum, the Palos Verdes peninsula provides a choice of diving spots that you can tour in a short time. You can check all four of them out with very little wasted motion. Whether your preference on a particular day is for solitude (Rocky Point) or for ease of access (White Point), you can find a good spot on this tour.

Catalina Island

Twenty-six miles out to sea from Los Angeles is beautiful, undeveloped Catalina Island. The diving on the protected side of the island is often extravagantly beautiful, with crystalline water, giant kelp, and a richness of marine animals. A dive trip to Catalina can be an exhilarating experience for beginners and old salts alike, but it entails the unavoidable problem of choosing a mode of transportation — unless, of course, you or your friends have a seagoing boat at your disposal. (If you are lucky enough to have use of such a boat, skip the next few pages — you are in business.)

For most of us, there are two types of transportation to Catalina: either public transportation from San Pedro, or private diving boats from San Pedro or Long Beach. The public transportation consists of the steamship from San Pedro to Avalon and the seaplane from San Pedro to Avalon. The steamship is cheap ($9.50 round trip at last check) but slow (two to three hours one way), while the plane is fast (20 minutes) but costs twice as much ($19.90 round trip). The problem with both is that their destination point, Avalon, is not a good diving area. Avalon is a tourist area, capitalizing on wide sandy beaches that hold little interest for a diver. The diving spots are scattered among the rocky coves and points around the island. One way of reaching the really inspirational diving spots is to rent a skiff in Avalon and set out yourself. But to do this you must spend still more money, and you should have a knowledge of the coastal conditions. We do not recommend it for the first trip to Catalina. One other, perhaps cheaper, possibility is to bring a bicycle and camping gear on the ferry and pedal around the island scouting for promising dive spots.

Since private dive boats ferry divers and their equipment to and from selected dive spots on the Cataline coast, they are the best choice for your first trip. Some dive boats are owned by dive shops, but some are individually owned and chartered out to groups sponsored and arranged by dive shops. While most divers on any boat trip are scuba divers either out on a pleasure dive or taking a practice dive, the cost of the trip, ranging from $15 to $22 round trip, will be the same for you as a free diver. Since this is a substantial outlay, a couple of suggestions will help you get your money's worth from the trip.

First, shop around: Call all the dive shops in the phone book, ask for prices, times, destinations, and what kinds of groups use their boats. Also call the 22nd Street Landing, in San Pedro, where the dive boats are moored, to get the phone numbers of the skippers of the boats.

Whatever your choice of transportation, we suggest that you make the trip with a group of free divers, to provide company and to make certain that you will have a buddy at any time during the day's diving. Since you will be at the dive site for about six hours, having enough people assures that any one diver can find someone to go in with at any particular time. It can be pretty frustrating if you want to explore a particular rock while the only other free diver wants to settle into a long lunch.

Speaking of lunch, we strongly suggest you bring your own in a cooler. Most boats have a galley where you can buy hamburgers, potato chips, soft drinks, and often beer at moderately inflated prices, but you can probably do much better for yourself with a homemade picnic.

Finally, before you commit yourself to the trip, check the weather forecasts as well as dive shop reports about Catalina conditions. Since you're spending money for transportation, you should bide your time until diving conditions are most favorable. (In general, late summer and fall are the best times.) Also, the two-hour boat trip over and back can be miserable on a choppy and rolling sea.

Diving at Catalina can be spectacularly beautiful. One very popular spot is Emerald Bay, probably the best destination for your first trip. The dive boats anchor in shallow water (30 feet) near large rock formations that shelter an extraordinary variety of underwater life.

The rich, very shallow areas around the rocks are great exploring. While the conventional wisdom is that Emerald Bay has been "picked over" and "fished out," as a free diver you can find abalone and lobster right around the protruding rock formations. Just remember that you will have the most success in crevices where the masses of scuba divers cannot reach.

When the water is good and clear (and you will have checked recent reports to make sure it is) you can see "indefinitely" — the giant kelp rising gracefully to the surface, schools of bright subtropical fish, and massive rock formations covered with algae and seaweed of all colors. Feel free to take along your spear and your abalone iron; but the underwater scenery is so entrancing you'll find it hard to concentrate on hunting. The first trip can easily be passed in discovering and exploring the variety of plants and animals. Look for abalone and keyhole limpets under rocks. Holes and crevices often conceal lobsters or eels or both, but neither will bother a diver unless he physically interferes with the animal; mere observation, even at very close range, will not provoke an eel. Although not really friendly in any sense; these creatures are not dangerous. The rocky areas also harbor small octopuses, which are quite shy and harmless. And the varieties of fish are beyond cataloging here.

In sum, the trip to Catalina is a thrilling experience, if the potential problems of transportation and water conditions are planned for carefully.

SAN DIEGO AREA DIVE SPOTS

The La Jolla Cove area is an exceptionally good spot for divers of all levels of skill and any interests.

71

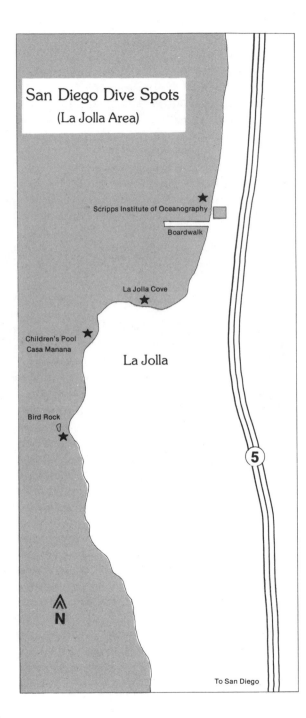

San Diego Dive Spots
(La Jolla Area)

Scripps Institute of Oceanography

Boardwalk

La Jolla Cove

Children's Pool
Casa Manana

La Jolla

Bird Rock

N

To San Diego

In no sense is it a place where you merely learn and then leave to move on to better things. However, to satisfy your natural appetite for variety, several other dive spots can be found on the La Jolla shoreline, one of them in San Diego itself.

Children's Beach – Casa Manana

If you follow the shoreline boulevard south from La Jolla Cove for a half mile, guiding yourself by the bike path signs, you will soon arrive at another dive spot. It looks like a miniature harbor, about the size of the Cove, complete with a very small jetty, all dominated by a lifeguard tower right out of *Star Trek*. Officially known as "the Children's Pool," and unofficially known to the local surf gangs as "Casa," this area is a very good place to dive for several reasons. While a good westerly wind will form big, mean-looking breakers at the tip of the jetty, reducing to a few square yards the area of calm waters suitable for neophytes, on a calm day it is almost as good a place as the Cove for beginners. And you might ignore the architecture of the lifeguard tower and walk right in to ask for information. The lifeguards, employed by the city, are mostly surfers and ex-surfers and they tend to be very observant and knowledgeable about sea conditions, including forecasting and visibility. Their science-fiction tower is an excellent observation post. We have always found them friendly and helpful with information but free of the mother hen tendencies of so many lifeguards.

But the main attraction of a dive at Children's Beach is that one of the branches of the very deep San Diego Marine Canyon runs alongside it. Because only a few hundred feet directly outside the jetty and parallel to it, the bottom drops abruptly to great depths, the area is frequented by very large fish not usually found in shallow waters, including the great White Bass. This spot also has very large lobsters, but unfortunately they seem to dwell a little deeper than elsewhere in La Jolla. The Marine Canyon's proximity to the Children's Pool may give rise to unanticipated encounters. In fact, the only time we saw a giant squid was right there. It may have measured about six feet from tip to tip but it was very dead — which is just as well because to cook it we would have needed the boiler of an old locomotive.

Surfers' Beach

Still continuing south, you leave the shore for a couple of miles and detour, still following the bike path signs until you return to the shore and reach a long stretch of narrow, sandy beach. This is the most frequented public beach in La Jolla, and as you might guess from its name, it also has the favor of surfers. Since it is completely open to westerly winds, it tends to be a little rough on a windy day. On this beach, any rocky outcroppings more than 100 yards off the high tide line are good for perch and some lobsters. The last outcropping at the extreme southern end of the beach is usually covered by long, rolling surf and is difficult to reach. But on a calm day, it is an incredible lobster haven, with bugs only three and four feet below the surface in the horizontal cracks that run parallel to the shore. They seem to make a good living by just sitting there and letting the surf bring them their daily bread. Occasionally, schools of jacks will wander into the area. In the summer, there are also small schools of little squids swimming near the surface, but we haven't yet found a way to catch them.

Parallel to Surfer's Beach, about one or one and a half miles out, is a very large band of giant kelp. It abounds with large fishes of several species, including barracuda and yellow tail, in season. Unfortunately, it also shelters some sharks, a few of which might just have evil intentions. Don't let yourself be tempted, at least not without a boat.

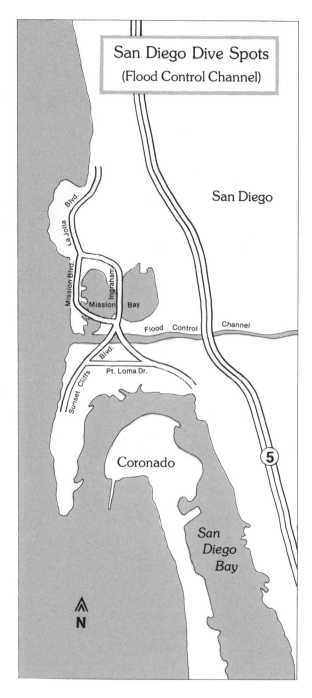

Children's Beach across from Casa Manova near downtown La Jolla is a good diving spot.

Bird Rock

A couple of miles south of Surfer's Beach is Bird Rock, a tall rock outcropping about 100 yards from the shore. There is direct access from the small parking area at the foot of Bird Rock Road. The Bird Rock area does not have a particularly attractive underwater terrain. It is strewn with big boulders and is kind of grassy. But it is usually fairly calm when other, more exposed spots are rough. It offers small lobsters in shallow waters and some green abalone, but not in sufficient quantity to explain why local people so favor this area. Perhaps it shows once again how incredibly conservative divers can be; generation after generation, divers will hit the same spots that were once good. Or perhaps local divers know something about Bird Rock we don't know. Try it after the other spots mentioned here, and decide for yourself. Note, though, that this is not a good place to be accompanied by nondivers

since there is really no comfortable place to sit on the shore.

Scripps Marine Institute

If you want to try your hand at some pretty subtle hunting, you might consider retracing your steps and turning toward the opposite, northern end of La Jolla. Let the modern buildings of the new U.C. San Diego campus, standing high on the cliff, be your beacon. Slightly below and before the University are the grey unassuming buildings of the World famous Scripps Oceanographic Institute (whose aquarium is well worth a visit). Scripps is marked on the sea side by a huge wharf extending far into the ocean. Both U.C. San Diego and Scripps are separated from the previously mentioned southerly spots by a very wide nonpublic beach that seems to be controlled by a private club. No need to bitch about all this wasted space; it's all sandy and probably sterile. You may *not* dive at Scripps itself, but you may get to the sea through its gardens, which are public. Walk on the sandy beach to the north of the wharf, until you reach the foot of a very steep cliff covered by huge boulders. Once there, any place is as good as any other.

We refer to this part of the La Jolla coastline as one for subtle hunting and we mention it last because it offers strange, all-or-nothing conditions. Its terrain is a combination of very fine white sands and rocky outcroppings. It offers a perfect hiding habitat for all the free swimming mimetic fishes. We have bagged different kinds of jacks there on several occasions, and we once saw (and missed) a school of barracuda. The area also has plenty of halibut, some small rock scallops, and a few exiled lobsters. We have often come back from Scripps empty handed even though it undeniably has fish. You might want to try it after several days of diving in La Jolla, when you have become sick and tired of not being able to stick your head under water without being confronted by an ugly, grimacing lobster.

Flood Control Channel

The flood control channel at the mouth of the San Diego River is an unusual dive spot. You can park on the access road on the north side of the channel or in the recreation area on the south side. The habitat between the rocky manmade channel walls has attracted great numbers of *nudibranchs*, or shell-less snails. You can spot specimens up to six inches long, banded with vivid blue and brown or yellow and brown stripes, plodding around the sandy bottom.

The flood control channel is usually very calm, with acceptable visibility. The only area deep enough to dive is between the Mission Bay Drive bridge and the ocean outlet. You enter from the rocky shore and swim out toward the middle, where depth reaches 10 to 15 feet. Much of the bottom is covered with light green vegetation that looks exactly like lettuce. In the sandy patches, you should look for the nudibranchs crawling about their business, and for flatfishes nestled in the sand. In the middle of the channel, nearer the bridge than the ocean outlet, is a rocky reef where more fish congregate. This untroubled body of water is also said to harbor small octopuses, although we have not seen any. The attraction of the flood control channel is a marine habitat thoroughly different from the rocky coast of La Jolla, as well as calm water and ease of access. The more you become an underwater naturalist, the more you will enjoy diving there.

8 WHAT TO CATCH AND WHERE

Just as there is no way to morally justify to everyone the enterprise of becoming a good predator, there is no way to fully describe its delights. The predatory instinct in modern man seems to be deeply rooted in the dim past of prehistoric man. And modern man, if he rationally pursues available game, is doing himself or his family the same service his hunting ancestors performed — providing food for the table. So the diver who hunts is satisfying some deep but constantly frustrated instinctive need, is learning his own competence and seeing its growth, and is getting healthful exercise as well.

Thus, to those among the ecology-minded who are misguided enough to believe that divers who fish are practiced in cruelty and are destroying the ecological balance, we utter a firm denial. Cruelty plays no role (or only a counterproductive one which we will mention later). And a free diver acting rationally — that is, according to his own self-interest — makes no perceptible dent in the ecology of any area: He is not effective enough for that. On the other hand, a collection of lazy, unimaginative divers are quite capable of quickly depopulating a *particular, small* spot. Thus, it is quite believable that Northern California's "good abalone spots" of yesteryear have been decimated by the dozens of divers who hit them weekend after weekend. But very often, a hundred yards to the right or left of the barren spot, abalone are climbing all over each other for lack of room.

As strange as it may sound, believing that the modern diver is practicing his own version of ancestral skills helps in becoming a good underwater fisherman. Placing squarely the responsibility for success and failure on the diver's competence eliminates the temptation to believe in magic: "Luck" is one form of magic, as is its opposite, "the empty ocean complex"; "quality of equipment" is another, more perverse form because it has an element of truth. Thinking in terms of competence also gives you the patience to learn: Your competence can only increase with each dive, it can't regress or abandon you as "luck" does. An experienced fishing diver will take one look at a section of shoreline, tell you what he is going to catch, and more often than not bring it back. But don't let that overimpress you. The more you dive, the faster you will be able to do the same, in fact, quite fast — that is, if you don't allow yourself to be discouraged by what you will see on the first few dives, for what you will see will be very little.

If you are in Northern California, the water will sometimes be murky and you will barely distinguish strands of kelp in the midst of the murk. In Southern waters, which are clearer, you will be pleased by the abundant flora and by the spectacle of hundreds of small fish that will all be too small to shoot. That's because it takes a little while to learn how to see in a strange environment governed by different rules than those on dry land. On land, the larger and the more mobile an object, the more visible it is and the less you have to scan to notice it. We are so used

The tiny convict fish is too small to eat, but a delight to watch.

to this that we think of it as somehow "natural." In the sea, the reverse tends to be true: Large mobile creatures become large by sagaciously using their mobility to get out of the way or to pounce, as the case may be; big fish and shellfish both conceal themselves carefully in order to become large. Remember that all sea creatures practice to an extraordinary degree the art of camouflage; the most spectacular artists, like the octopus, can switch in two seconds from a perfect imitation of red rock and green seaweed to white sand. Large rockfish seem to know how they can avoid detection while in a hole by placing themselves in such a way that the refracted sun rays blind any nosy predator. Halibut and flounder cover themselves entirely with sand. Perhaps most impressive of all, some species of carnivorous fish can float motionless in perfectly clear water and become so transparent that the diver fails to see them until he gets so close that they dart right under his nose.

This brief warning should be enough to let you guess that you can't compete in this tricky, wondrous world with your eyes alone. Fortunately, you have a couple of aces in your game that sea creatures do not suspect: After a while you learn their rather predictable habits and you can guess where they ought to be. If they play by the rules, your eyes, forwarned, detect them. If they don't try elsewhere!

When you begin to seek out information about fishing areas, you will quickly discover that nobody seems to know much. The surface fisherman's information is almost useless to divers beyond telling them what game inhabits a given large area. Sunday anglers who think on too small a scale; professional fishermen, who are a thousand times more mobile, operate on much too vast a scale.

Local divers are usually very specialized and tradition bound. Though they are your best source of information, they are an additional cause of scarcity of information: Those who know something don't like to tell. We remember asking a La Jolla diver whether there could be lobster in a particular small section of shoreline; he answered that no one had taken a lobster there in 10 years. Skeptical, we went in anyway and caught several nice size "bugs" in a half-hour.

If you don't have any knowledgeable, trustworthy friends, your best bet is probably the local dive shop owner. He sees and listens to more divers than anyone else and it is to his interest to detain you in his area and to make you come back for more.

In the meantime, we would like to give you some bits and pieces of our own fishing lore. This information is not to be used literally and slavishly like a car owner's manual; it is certainly not the whole picture, or perhaps even most of the picture, about each species. But our observations and suggestions provide a reliable and tested part of the picture. (Some of the best game fish in California, such as black sea bass, will not be mentioned here because they are beyond the capability of virtually all free divers, ourselves included.)

The sea hunter makes his first, basic distinction between sea life that moves and sea life that doesn't. To catch a sedentary creature, the diver need rely only on an understanding of its habitat; to catch moving prey he must also rely on skill and timing.

Mobile Game

The diver's mobile game are fish and crustaceans. Fish can be further classified as free swimming fish, rock fish and flat fish. Certain types of free swimming fish flee when confronted by a diver, and others merely hide nearby. Fleeing fish are usually carnivorous, long and thin, silvery, and have small scales. They include white bass, barracuda (seen only in Southern California and seldom even there), jacks of all kinds, mullet, mackerels, and some tuna-like species such as the yellow tail. They are the prize game for the hunter and the diver. But the wariness of such fish makes them hard to see and even harder to approach. Most carnivorous fish tend to swim close to the surface, sometimes in the surf, especially at sunup and sundown. They like to spend the day motionless, hidden in the weeds on the bottom. During their hours of activity you will find them toward the ocean side of exposed rocks, riding the rip current created by the splashing of sea on rock. Sometimes — particularly when schools of small fish such as smelt are around (watch the cormorants*) — they can be seen in the breakers of very shallow water, down to three or four feet. Look around also when you find yourself in an area where a body of warm water meets a cold current or vice versa; they seem to favor such places, perhaps because they offer a happy compromise between keeping warm and getting high on oxygen (which cold water carries more of than warm water).

Fleeing fish are extraordinarily sensitive to anything that smacks of threatening behavior. The trick is to approach them at an angle while pretending that they don't exist. We know that biologists will drub us for this, but we are convinced that these fish are able to detect our blood-letting intentions by the vibes we broadcast into the water. Moreover, they seem to know what a speargun is — at least they are aware of significant differences between the behavior of armed and unarmed divers.** An experienced French diver who is a perennial spearfishing champion contends that they can perceive the killer's look in the diver's eyes. To conceal his eyes, he made himself a face mask with a glass plate that is a one-way mirror.

Yet, these open water fish have a fatal flaw. Since they make their living by being curious of any possible prey, they can't resist the temptation to investigate any small noises or small tremors or whatever might indicate the proximity of a wounded creature. Needless to say, they lose some of their restraint when tantalized by a dead fish at the end of a line tied to a diver's belt. Telling you more would be a grave betrayal of precious trade secrets; and we

*Ignore the gulls; they are very lazy birds, fishing only at last resort.
**In some places barracuda follow divers at a safe distance, suggesting that they have some idea of a speargun reach.

Fish respond to a friendly approach. They can distinguish an amiable wave of the hand from a speargun.

These southern California schooling fish are delicious, but they tend to vanish when an armed diver approaches.

are not sure that, even if we wanted to, we could describe the techniques used to attract these fish. Just believe that they can be *called* and develop your own method. Don't be in a hurry, though; they are the most difficult game to bag, are rather scarce at best, and are either nonexistent or invisible north of Santa Barbara. One last tip: Silvery, carnivorous fish should be thoroughly barbecued or baked with a minimum of spices and accompanied by a light, very dry white wine.

The length of the California coast is blessed with giant kelp, which provides food, lodging, and entertainment for an enormous variety of perches, the most common hiding fish. Perches swim in small schools of 10 to 50 fish. They react only to frontal attacks and tend to return to their hangout a couple of minutes after going into hiding, usually behind the next strand of kelp. Perches are almost too easy to bag but they reproduce rather fast. After 10 years of intensive hunting weekend after weekend, the famous Monterey breakwater still carries a large population of perch. We prefer the silver-colored "butter mouth" perch, because it resembles most the fleeing fish in both behavior and taste.
both behavior and taste.

Perches are good cooked in any way: barbecued, baked or fried. Accompany them with a heavy white wine or a dry rose.

Where you find perch, you should also find other types of free swimming fish, such as sea trout, sheeps head, and kelp bass.

Practically any area that boasts of both kelp and a rocky bottom shelters a population of rockfish, more varied and plentiful in the north, sparser in the south. Rockfish have the peculiarity of living in holes on the bottom; they rarely come out except for a quick snack. This trait and their expertness at camouflage make them difficult to see unless you swim with your nose plowing the bottom, peering into every hole. It would be difficult to repeat this too often: A surprising number of divers, including experienced ones, underestimate the plentifulness of rockfish on an average California bottom. We

suspect that most such divers are handicapped by a certain repugnance to search the bottom and to stick their heads into holes. Is it possible that giant squid and sea monster stories die hard? The lingcod, for example, which is often considered the best Northern California catch, is reputedly scarce. In our experience, when lingcods are in season, at various times during the winter, depending on the area, 25 square feet of rocky bottom can conceal up to five or six of them. But while young lingcods often show curiosity and come out to investigate divers, most rockfish, including cabezon and rockcod, remain unbudging in their holes. This makes them a little difficult to find but, once detected, very easy to shoot. Except for large lingcods, most rockfish don't put up a fight when shot. But rockfish have soft flesh; though they are easy to shoot, they are difficult to retrieve because they tend to tear away from the shaft. Make sure your shaft head is very sharp. Shoot a rockfish "from the hip," as soon as you see it. It will recede deeper into its hole as soon as *it* sees you.

Some connoisseurs love rockfish fillets fried in butter, and the Chinese bake them with sweet and sour sauce; but we don't consider them worthy of this kind of honor. On the other hand, they make an excellent fish soup, the greater the variety of species the better. Simmer a long time with onions, garlic, plenty of white wine, and fresh anise. Add a dash of Pernod before serving.

Rockfish have neither the silvery dash of carnivorous fish nor the characteristic rounded silhouette of perches. By and large, they are rather ugly fishes with quasiconical, spiny bodies. Lingcods and cabezons have unreasonably large heads and no scales. Their colors vary greatly depending on their habitats; lingcod coloring, for example, can go from bright South Sea blue to deep red, spotted or striped.

In the flatfish category, we place, contrary to proper scientific taxonomy, not only flounders, soles, and halibuts, but also rays and skates, because you will find all of them around the same

It's necessary to skim the bottom to catch rockfish and other bottom-dwellers.

The grumpy lingcod, a bottom-dweller is a prize catch in northern California.

bottoms. Halibut, flounder, the small sandab, and the rare soles are sometimes encountered on very sandy bottoms. They also live on mud, but since we never dive in such spots we can't say much about it. To this day, we haven't been able to develop a clear understanding of where and when to look for flounder and halibut. Many times we have looked for them in areas they were reputed to frequent, with no success. On the other hand, we caught several by chance when we had strayed over sandy bottoms while looking for other fish (this always south of San Francisco). Flounder and halibut are difficult to see because they at once bury themselves in the sand and adjust their colors and markings to that sand. Usually, they can only be detected by the relief of their oblong shape, which shows even when they are completely buried under a fine layer of sand. Strike as soon as you see them: Both their eyes are on top of their heads and they will see you at least as soon as you see them; they will flee for about 20 to 50 yards, describing a fairly flat arc before returning to rest in the sand.

Flatfish are easily caught with a handspear because they can be pinned to the ocean floor. Remember, though, that halibut can reach 60 pounds! They seem to be fond of sandy areas next to low-lying rocks. We have seen them in both very deep and very shallow waters.

All the true flatfish are excellent eating, perhaps the best of fish. Using no spices, bake, barbecue or pan fry in butter depending on size.

Sand dabs and soles are probably too small to find, and we have never caught any.

Rays and skates abound on sandy bottoms, as well as in other places. They cannot be mistaken for flounder or halibut because they are either clearly diamond shaped or nearly circular and both have long, wispy tails. The stingray carries an ugly, poisonous barb at the *base* of its tail. Leave stingrays alone and they will leave you alone. In general, we leave rays and skates alone because they are sluggish, a little dumb, and not particularly good to eat. Resist the temptation of trophy hunting in spite of

the fact that rays often top 100 pounds.

Crustaceans are found up and down the length of the coast. Northern California has several varieties of edible crabs, most of which can also be found in the South, though in lesser numbers.

Wherever you find rock formations resting on sand, you are likely to also find rock crabs if you look underneath the rocky overhangs in the soft sand bed. These crabs are nicknamed "sleeper crabs" because they often dwell in the intertidal zone, letting themselves be stranded high and dry by an ebbing tide and simply napping under a rock until the next high tide. The top of the sleeper crab's carapace is dark brown and maroon, and its underside always has red dots, as do its foreclaws. Their bodies, about the size of your hand, are thick and sturdy, with short stout pincers. These rock crabs are scientifically known as *Cancer Antennarius*. In this instance, formal taxonomy is good to know because there are no Fish and Game regulations governing size and bag limits for the rock crab, while there are rules about the market crab, *(Cancer Magister)*, a similar but somewhat larger crab whose habitat sometimes overlaps with that of the rock crab. The market crab has a wider span, slimmer body, and longer forepincers. Its carapace is usually a brighter red than the rock crab's. Various kinds of spider crabs, which look like miniature Alaskan king crabs, are also found, but their spindly limbs don't contain enough meat to make them a worthwhile catch.

Crabs can be caught with a line or trap, or by hand while either diving or shore picking. The ideal way to approach any crab is to dive right on top of it and seize it with one hand right behind its large claws. Held that way, it can't pinch you. Since crabs are more often resting in the deepest recess of a crack then running around on the bottom, you need to know other techniques. One technique is to catch both pinchers at once, one in each hand, and to keep them apart while swimming. While this effectively immobilizes the creature, it requires that you balance yourself without using your hands. Unless the weights on your belt are scientifically spread,

You can shore pick for crabs at low tide even when the ocean is rough. Reach under a rock ledge and feel around in the sand for a sleeping crab.

Pull the crab out by whatever you can get hold of. Once out, it attempts to activate its pincers.

This tasty specimen is a male. You can tell by the narrow triangular strip on his stomach. Females have a wider and hairier one. Plan to catch two crabs this size for each person at dinner.

Here is the rock crab blissfully asleep underwater, with its pincers tucked safely underneath.

there is little chance that you can use this method. The next technique requires blind faith (in us), because a large crab can inflict very painful wounds indeed. We believe that crabs don't have a very good sense of balance and lose their cool very easily. Therefore, simply catch the animal by one pincher and shake the hell out of it from the minute you grasp it to the moment it is safely in your catchbag. Losing its footing when you pull it out, your victim gets worried and tries so desperately to regain footing that it forgets to pinch you. Try it with small crabs first.

We have developed a crab lure to make diving for crabs a more reliable source of dinner. Take three or four metal weights of about two pounds each and tie them four feet apart on a 20-foot long rope. Tie some crab bait very securely to each of the metal weights. Our favorite bait is chicken necks, but crabs will try most types of fish or meat scraps. Attach a float of some sort (an empty plastic bottle is good) to the long end of the rope. Take the whole apparatus out to where you think crabs live, lay the metal weights along the bottom, and let the float rise toward the surface so that you can find the spot again. Go dive somewhere else for ten minutes, and you should return to find groups of crabs jostling for your bait. Dive down and grab them from behind. We have noticed that possession of the bait usually falls to relatively large male crabs, which make a better catch.

Crabbing by hand can also be done at low tides, when the mixed rock and sandy areas are uncovered. Just reach under a rock or rock ledge and feel around in the sandy bottom. When you feel a hard object half buried in the sand, pull it out, get a good grip on it from behind the pincers, and stick it in your bag.

Crabs are very territorial animals and hate each other's guts. Several crabs thrown together in the same bag will immediately engage in a battle to the finish. In order to bring them back alive, stuff a lot of kelp in your bag just as soon as you can. Your catch will use it to screen themselves from their neigh-

bors, and will get from it some of the humid air they need. If you must wait a long time before cooking your catch, place it in a bag and sprinkle it with a can of beer or some wine. The animals will get nicely drunk and go to sleep, thereby not exhausting their precious flesh. (This also works on lobster.)

Crabs are so easy to catch that you have no excuse for taking females, which have small pinchers anyway, and are therefore a less desirable meal. Learn to recognize them; they have a wider, hairier abdomen. Anything that lays eggs is a female.

Crabs must be boiled or steamed alive for 15 or 20 minutes. If you have many, cook several batches in the same water. The stuff left in the water by the first batch will help preserve the taste of the second batch. Sprinkle lemon on the meat and drink beer or white wine with it.

Southern California's rocky areas are graced and redeemed by the teeming hosts of spiny lobsters they shelter. The spiny lobster differs in a major way from its North Atlantic "Maine" cousin: Its pinchers are underdeveloped while its overgrown antennas are its main defense; it is pink to red to brown instead of blue. Its flesh, which is just as exquisite as its cousin's, makes it the prize of prizes, though the spiny lobster is a bottom feeder that will eat absolutely anything. Where there is any lobster, there is lots of it: If you find one lobster in one spot or if you see somebody catch one in a particular spot, keep looking; there are bound to be more around.

According to marine biologists, there is no lobster of any kind north of Point Conception. Though we have never had occasion to contradict them with facts, we have been haunted by the strong suspicion that large bugs let themselves be carried much farther north by coastal currents. By and large, any *rocky* area south of Santa Barbara is likely to have some lobster. The Channel Islands and islands in general are particularly good bets, and of course most of the San Diego coastline is teeming with lobster — including, practically, downtown La Jolla.

Here is a family of spiny lobsters gathered just outside their rocky shelter. Grab the big one.

Now, if you had a formidable head covered with spines, you had a relatively softer back end, and you loathed to work for your living, what kind of ocean spot would you look for? You would look for a horizontal crack, fairly deep and facing the surf. You would lodge your soft tail end snugly against the narrow end of the crack and sit contentedly waiting for the motions of the sea to bring you your daily ration of debris. That is exactly what most lobsters usually do. You will find them in small bands of three or four under ridges, usually in the deepest recesses but sometimes in such shallow holes that their antennas are showing. Another good bet is the largest holes under piles of big boulders well exposed to surf action. (Look for crumbled cliffs in deep water and search the water underneath them). The third most likely place to look for lobster, in our experience, is under a single large rock sitting on a sandy bottom. They seem to like sitting on the sand with their tops well protected by a solid rock ceil-

86

ing. On a few occasions, we have seen a full crown of antennas emerging from underneath a boulder. According to Southern California divers, lobsters go out at night and crawl around on the bottom. Also, remember that they leave a perfect shell behind when they molt. An empty shell is a sure sign that something is happening very near.

Garibaldi, which look exactly like oversized, bright red goldfish (and which, by the way, are legally protected) will often dart straight for a lobster hole when scared. Follow them. And yes, it is true, lobster lairs sometimes also shelter a moray eel. But if you can see the lobster, you can see the eel and choose the wisest course, which consists of *not* matching your soft fingers against its sharp teeth.

Catching lobster should be easy because, frankly, they are a little dumb; when they see you, they are as likely to take a few steps toward you as anything else. Nevertheless, each bug will probably give you

This lobster is ready to be dropped into the pot.

a lot of work, even after you learn how to find them. For one thing, the law requires that you take them by hand, and many lobster holes are much too deep and narrow for this. Though in very rough areas you will find some lobsters in shallow water (10 feet), they ordinarily prefer some depth (20 feet). So, you will have to reach out and make a grab in a very short time before you must come up for air. Finally, though they will let you come very close, once they understand intentions they can move incredibly fast, forward, backward, and sideways. But if one darts, don't give up. Chances are that you will find it in the nearest suitable hole, usually less than 10 feet away.

There is really no good way to grab a normally positioned bug that is facing you. Wearing a garden glove helps, because when seized it will try to pinch your hand between its sharp antennas and its thorny back. If you can (and you can very rarely), try to slip your hand *underneath* it. It will grab with its legs,

but these are harmless. Pulling a lobster by its antennas does not work because it will allow them to break off rather than surrender. Once you hold the beast, shove it in a bag and don't open it except briefly to give it a roommate. Use a piece of antenna to remove the intestine through the anus lest the flesh become bitter.

There are a thousand sophisticated ways to prepare lobster, most of them too specialized to describe here. If you don't want to get into the real science of it, just remember the following principles: Like crab, lobster should be cooked alive with its shell intact. If any part of the shell is damaged, broil it rather than boil it. Small lobsters take well to being cast alive in heavily salted, hard-boiling water; larger ones are better tied up and broiled in a hot oven. All lobsters are delicious barbecued. Split them down the middle, spread melted butter on them, and place them close to a very low, flameless fire of charcoal. Eat every part — tail, head, and legs — accompanied by a slightly fruity white wine or, of course, dry champagne.

A note on mobile game and sunlight: It is true, as many pole fishermen will tell you, that most mobile sea creatures know a period of intense activity at sunrise and another one at sunset. Try to take advantage of these if it is convenient, but don't let anyone tell you that it is impossible to catch this or that creature in the middle of the day. They all have to spend the day somewhere.

In some respects, the middle of the day is the best time to dive because the sunrays then reach farthest and give you the best visibility. They can also blind you and cause you to cast a shadow. Try, if the relief allows it, to alternate between one drawback and the other.

Immobile Game

The pride, joy, and greed of the California diver lies with the abalone. The abalone is God's own reward and sign of special approval to the only members of the human race who will voluntarily and regularly immerse themselves in cold, murky waters. Mediterranean and tropical divers get limpid waters and limitless vistas, but only *we* get the abalone. Though there are many stories circulating among biologists and in the media about the depletion of this gift of God, we can assure you that it is still extremely plentiful along most of the California coast. The scare stories are probably spread by discouraged amateurs, and by disgruntled commercial divers who would like to see resumption of the "harvesting" of the sea otter (supposed to be the commercial diver's rival). Marine biologists who join in the chorus have probably forgotten a leaf of their undergraduate textbook. Organisms first respond to being heavily collected not by disappearing but by adapting. The relatively versatile abalone has probably adapted to the new environmental fact of abalone catchers simply by living at greater depths. Consider the now-common story of how in

the old days Portuguese farmers used to go collect abalone on Sunday morning in their church clothes "without so much as wetting their shoes, sir." Abalone became wise, evolutionarily speaking, to this sort of practice and moved down below, where it is too cold and wet for one's Sunday best. In Western France, where a smaller species is found, this is exactly what took place. Abalone can be found there by the dozens about three feet *below* the lowest tideline, where they are safe from shore pickers. This retreat to a lower depth corresponds roughly with the post-World War II rise in the French standard of living, which multiplied tenfold the number of seacoast vacationers and, of course, fishing enthusiasts.

If California biologists dived in larger numbers, they would soon convince themselves that abalone, *as a species*, are not threatened though in some specific locations populations may have dwindled. In any case, the current bag limit of five (which is rigidly enforced) seems to us perfectly reasonable. Five abalone is enough to give very large families of very great gluttons a nice Sunday dinner — a meal that no restaurant offers at *any* price.

Alarm over the supposedly dwindling number of abalone remaining on our coasts may have been amplified by the knowledge that, in fact, abalone is very easy to catch once you know how. It hardly moves around and any diver worth his salt knows that any time the ocean is not too rough to dive, he can catch his dinner. Yet, probably hundreds of people, all fired up by their desire for that exquisite taste, have taken lessons and have bought equipment only to give up after a dozen dives without having so much as seen a live abalone. The reason for this is simple: In catching abalone, everything is in the eye and in blind faith (no play on words). The abalone is the most perfect illustration we know of the uncapriciousness of nature: Any area that, according to a few simple criteria, should have abalone, does have them. And a sighted abalone is a cooked abalone. Here are the criteria. The underwater terrain must be rocky and jagged with a minimum of sand and no mud. The larger (up to 10 inches) red abalone that range south to Point Conception will most often be found in horizontal cracks if in stratified terrain (slates), in vertical crevices and inside holes between granitic and sandstone boulders. Any place that has beds of floating giant kelp is sure to have some abalone, since kelp will attach itself to the kind of rocky bottom that abalone uses for protection. Abalone spots normally get a lot of surf action and are normally covered by rough waters. Abalone are strictly herbivorous: No seaweed, no abalone.

Red abalone always live in groups: If you have spotted one, look around, there are from two to 50 more in the immediate vicinity. Now, the problem of spotting an abalone is the source of all the heartbreak. Your normal hedonistic abalone will crawl around very, very slowly when seeking greener pastures. As a result, its thick, hard shell will provide support as good as a rock for absolutely anything that cares to grow on it: Small sponges, sea anemones, moss, algae in a mixture identical to the surroundings. Once we found a rock scallop growing on a live abalone shell. When it is unwary, the abalone will be "standing" on its foot, its shell two or more inches from the rock to which it clings and showing a lot of flesh. As soon as it senses any unusual vibes, it will flatten itself against its rock, leaving only a few miniature tentacles extended and blending with the rock surface.

There are two cardinal rules, respect of which make or break the abalone diver:

Find out approximately where this beautiful abalone colony will be *before* you enter the water. This can be done, with a little experience, if you only remember that underwater terrain is usually a simple extension of what is above water.

Stick your head right next to the rock surface you are prospecting. If the rubber border around the face plate of your mask does not get scratched once in a while, you are not doing it right. In the murky waters of Northern California, where the red abalone is most plentiful, you can only see an abalone when you are close enough to grab it, or, actually, too close (that is, with your face on it).

If you come close enough to an abalone without its sensing your presence, it is actually possible to jerk it off its rock with bare hands. However, they usually see you about the same time you see them and clamp down on their support. That's why it is normally necessary to use an abalone iron. Insert it anywhere between rock surface and abalone and pry the abalone loose. This gesture is easily learned, and, contrary to legend, abalone do not have tremendous strength. They will oppose about the same resistance as the suction of an average size plumber's helper. If you are worried, practice with one. Most divers who find it hard to pry an abalone loose are not weighted enough, so the force they exert tends to move them rather than the shellfish. (In fact, divers do not in general carry enough weight on their belts.)

You will hear many hair-raising stories about the great depths at which abalone perversely conceal themselves. Consider them part of the hairy chest mystique and poor attempts at self aggrandizement. Diving deep is no big deal; it's what you do down below that goes on your record. If you choose your spots as sagely as we advise, you will never have to go down below 20 feet to get your limit; 10 to 12 feet is normal. This brings us to the matter of tides in general and "good tides" and "bad tides" in particular.

If you drive along Highway 1 on one of the lowest tides of the year, you will see hundreds of divers in little groups of three or four, feverishly dressing up to be in the water well before it reaches its lowest point. If the tide is a particularly "good" one (that is, low) and if it happens to be low at four o'clock in the morning, the amazing thing is that you will witness exactly the same spectacle as at three in the afternoon. We at first followed this practice with the quasi-religious fear in our hearts that all the good abalone would be gone if we did not stick to a military schedule. But we grossly overslept a few

When looking for abalone, you have to pick your exact spot by intuition or experience.

Put your facemask up to the rocks to find an abalone. Get your iron underneath and pop it off.

This one is ready to go into the sack attached to the innertube float.

The crevice under the fish looks like a potential abalone spot, but the sea urchins have preempted it.

times, missed the low, low tide and went in anyway, while everyone else was walking back carrying more or less heavy loads. *We found that it did not make any appreciable difference in our results.* Because most good abalone spots go down pretty steeply, the difference in water level between an average tide and the lowest low tide could not be more than three or four feet. On the other hand, it is best to enter that cold water well-rested, after a full night's sleep and with a sunny sky overhead. Don't spoil your fun by doing something unnatural, like getting up at the hour at which you usually bed down, just to catch a tide. On the other hand, the water tends to be a little bit clearer when the tide is either fully down or fully up. Yet so many other factors affect water clarity so much more (storms in Japan, for example) that you should not let considerations of the tide limit your diving.

What we have said at length about the red abalone, which is the largest species, also applies to the green abalone, which is more sparse and tends to be found farther south though its range overlaps considerably with that of its red cousin. Green abalone is really green of skin. With a maximum spread of 8 inches, it is somewhat smaller than its red cousin but rather easier to find: Because the warmer waters in which it often lives do not support such a rich sea life, it carries fewer growths on its back and can be detected from a longer distance as a clear grey spot. (This is helped also by the greater visibility offered by Southern water.) Though it chooses its lodgings pretty much the same way the red abalone does, it is more likely than the latter to stick to the bottom of an underwater cliff.

Most abalone occupy the lowest, deepest points they can find on a given piece of sea bottom. This is true whether the average depth of this area is 10 or 30 feet. A notable exception is the black abalone, which is perhaps the single most visible species in California. It often lives on the same rocks as the two other species but at higher elevations.* It is still very common to find it exposed at low tide. It is much smaller (up to 5 inches) than the others and considerably tougher. We don't really think it is worth diving for, especially since it rarely reaches legal size.

Now we must approach the all-important topic of food preparation — all-important because it is very easy to spoil abalone, as most restaurants do. Moreover, unless you develop some traditions early, you will soon find yourself limiting your catch and even your diving in order to avoid the wearisome task of preparing your game. Preparing abalone for dinner is a wonderful ceremony: Sit in the sun, at the beach or back home, with divers and friends, and while away the evening's chores in a leisurely fashion. Don't treat it like work; it is the most dignified of human activities, a prelude to the transformation of the sea's noble gift into our own substance. The preparation itself is composed of three phases, which can be apportioned among the members of the party according to their abilities.

First, the living animal must be pried loose from its shell and the viscera separated from the muscle which alone is edible. The first operation is performed by inserting an abalone iron (or screwdriver) as far as possible between flesh and shell at the smaller end. Then, by a lever action, the flesh is torn from its attachment point in the hollow of the shell. When this is done, slip a hand right under the muscle at the wide end of the beast and pull upward while holding the shell down with the other hand. If properly executed, this maneuver should leave you holding almost pure muscle in your right hand, your left hand holding the shell still containing the viscera.

The second step, cutting and slicing, is critical because the eating tenderness of the flesh *un*obviously depends on it. The trick is to remorselessly cut off all the outer, dark parts until only about one-half the original muscle is left. This hurts because it looks like waste, but it is strictly necessary since the outer layers of flesh are very tough and are not improved by pounding. Besides, the cast-off parts can be used in a soup, Chinese style, or can be ground up to make patties, or can provide

*We know a specific rock on the San Mateo coast, the lower reaches of which are occupied by red abalones. Higher up, it forms a cave that shelters rock scallops, the highest stratum being studded with dozens of black abalones.

Five abalones – the legal limit – safely on shore.

Remove the abalone from its shell by inserting your iron as a wedge at the relatively pointed, "non-whorled" end.

an excellent high-protein meal for your pet, who will love it. Once cut down to size, the meat should be sliced as thin as possible. It is mandatory to have a very sharp knife.

The third stage is the well-known practice of pounding the slices to tenderize them; abalone meat is just too tough to be eaten without pounding. The best practice is to slip one or two slices into a plastic bag that is kept closed with one hand while you pound the meat inside it with a mallet held in the other. *Pound on a hard surface,* like concrete or stone, not on wood, which bounces. Pound it to a mushy consistency, until the slice of abalone resembles a Dali watch.

Once you have a respectable pile of well-pounded slices, start thinking about cooking and serving it right away. (Most restaurants waste this excellent flesh in two ways: by overbreading it (to save on meat) and by overcooking it. Having earned it so well through your hard work, you don't want to fall into such gross errors.) Dip each slice in salted beaten eggs, roll in bread crumbs, and throw into a *very hot* skillet containing about half an inch of previously heated oil or butter or both. Cook less than a minute on each side. *That is all.* Do not cook on a slow fire, do not put too many pieces in the skillet at once; this would lower the temperature. Serve with rice and salad. Drink only white wine or beer.

For a more elaborate version use the following recipe. Prepare the meat as just described, slicing and pounding into thin steaks, the larger and the more regular in circumference, the better. Prepare a batter of milk and eggs and have bread crumbs standing by. Saute thin slices of pepper — green pepper for ordinary people, and hot peppers for hot-pepper types. Grate a batch of mild cheese such as Monterey Jack. Place some peppers and cheese on a slice of abalone. Roll it into Tamale shape with pepper and cheese in the center, and fix shut with toothpicks. Roll the business in the batter and the crumbs. Deep fry in one inch of very hot oil for 25 seconds, *30 at the most.* Scoop it out with a spatula

and let it drain for a few seconds before serving.

Other recipes can be found in cookbooks, but these two are the easiest and probably the best. Another nice characteristic of abalone flesh is that it keeps remarkably well. You can refrigerate raw abalone meat for about a week, but it should not be cut up, just separated from shell and viscera, otherwise it will bleed and lose much of its taste. In the freezer compartment, well-washed abalone flesh, whether sliced and pounded or not, will conserve its fresh taste for several months.

Once the joys of the abalone search begin to pale and it starts to feel like a trip to the supermarket (no kidding, it does become that easy), it is a good idea to begin thinking about the rarer and more delicate scallop.

California has both bay (mobile) and rock (fixed) scallop, but only the rock scallop is likely to be encountered by the diver. The bay scallop, as its name indicates, lives in bays and estuaries that tend to be a little muddy and murky. In addition, the bay scallop is said to live at great depths only. We cannot verify this as we have never found any, though we have looked for it from time to time. If you live near a bay, it might be worth giving it a try.

The rock scallop hardly looks like its bay counterpart: It is very rough and irregular in outline and rather thicker. It somewhat resembles an oyster trying to look circular. Nevertheless, it usually bears the typical "shell" sign near its point of attachment.

The first few times we stumbled upon rock scallop, we were exploring unlikely spots for abalone. We have since verified that both its range and its location overlap somewhat with the red abalone's. While we had often heard it stated categorically that no rock scallop lives north of Monterey, the first ones we found were fairly far north on the San Mateo coast (about 30 miles south of San Francisco). Because we've found what looked like the same species, though smaller and more numerous, in La Jolla and in Morro Bay (right next to the crabs mentioned before), we suspect that the whole coast

You need a fairly sharp tool like an abalone iron or screwdriver to pry scallops out of their cracks.

is studded with small colonies of scallop. This is what you must look for: Scallops seem to like clear water, carrying less stuff in suspension than is normal for California. They tend to live in small colonies (up to 20 individuals) inside shallow recesses in rock walls. Generalizing from most of our finds, we conclude that they must have alot of surf action but cannot be directly exposed to crashing surf. Thus, in rough surf areas, they will most often attach themselves to the landward side of a rock or to rocks protected by a reef or oriented sideways to the surf.

Wherever they locate, they are never far from the lowest tideline — that is, much higher up than abalone. Furthermore, we have found them in places almost always sandier and with much less vegetation than typical abalone sites. These facts plus the relative clarity of the water they frequent makes them fairly easy to spot. Their shells are normally clear grey and perfectly clean of any growth. As bivalves, they spend most of their time with their "mouths" open, exposing the bright red muscles inside.

They are very firmly attached to the rock surface; either the hinge end of the body or one whole side of the shell is cemented to the rock. This makes them difficult to sever, and, again, you should be well weighted to do it. The best implement is a fairly sharp "diver's tool"; this differs from a commercially sold abalone iron in that it is made of steel rather than aluminum and its extremity can be sharpened. A very large, heavy screwdriver could also be used.

Cookbooks abound in recipes (look under "Coquille Saint Jacques"). It's a major crime to take out just the main muscle and deep fry it. The whole inside is edible and excellent. We prefer them "au gratin," that is baked on their half shell covered with a mixture of minced onion, bread crumbs, milk, white wine, salt, pepper, and cheese. Serve very hot with light, dry, white wine.

The California coast has numerous other shellfish, clams and mussels in particular; but most of them either can be caught without diving or are nearly impossible to catch by diving. An exception is the big, beautiful Pismo clam. You dive for it armed with a garden trowel. Poke around in the sandy bottom. If you hit something hard, it's likely to be a Pismo clam. There are also several species of small oysters but they, like the bay scallop, live in estuaries where the water tends to be murky. Yet they are in shallow water and you might try for them if you are conveniently located.

Incidentally, mussels are very tasty and yet so often overlooked. You don't dive for them, but hand pick them at low tides. If you go to the beach for a picnic, nondivers can gather mussels. Put them in a closed pot with onion, celery and white wine. Cook until the mussel shells open. Extravagantly good! Observe the mussel quarantine from May to Nov. 1.

That, friends, is the extent of our knowledge at this point. Some of our information might be incomplete, even grossly so (we can never be sure that we have touched more than the edge of a species' range) but it is all accurate to the best of our knowledge. If you are never infected by gear fetishism or the hairy chest mystique, and you direct your efforts to learning, these few pages should help you cure yourself forever of the empty ocean complex. The sea is not only beautiful but also incredibly rich. Don't loot it. Strive to be just another predator; the joys of it are unlimited.

Since you have read this book to the end, there is no need to wish you good luck. Your ever-increasing competence will make it superfluous.

The goose barnacles in the foreground are not particularly good to eat, but the mussels (dark with scalloping on their shells) to the left are delicious.